Horse Racing Handicapping Books 1-4

By,

Bill Peterson

All this material is copyrighted ©. No reprint or copying without express, written consent of Bill Peterson and Willie's Publishing. ©2014

http://horse-racing-handicapping.co

The following material is meant for entertainment purposes only and is not an inducement to gamble. Wagering on horse racing in any form is gambling and therefore there is risk of loss.

If you or someone you know has a gambling problem, please contact Gamblers Anonymous at http://gamblersanonymous.org **or call their toll free number at** 888-GA-HELPS (888-424-3577)

Table of Contents

Section 1: 1

1. Horse Racing Long Shots, Red Flags, and Good Bet   1

2. Horse Racing Sight Handicapping For Winners Outside The Box   4

3. Horses Switching Distance May Be a Very Good Be   7

4. Horse Racing Angles and Suggestions For Better Wagering and More Wins   10

5. Trip Handicapping and What to Look For When Watching A Horse Race Replay   13

6. How To Handicap Horse Racing Workouts and Trainers   16

7. Long Shots, Sure Bets, and Everything In Between   19

8. The Top Four Horse Racing Handicapping Factors For Maiden Races   22

9. What Are The Best Odds To Bet On Thoroughbred Horses   25

10. What Horse Racing Videos Can Teach You and How They Help You To Win   28

11. Easy Handicapping Methods Based on the Tote Board Odd   31

12. Guaranteed-Can't Miss- a Bargain at Twice the Price- Horse Racing System For Big Profits and Lower Cholesterol   34

13. Horse Racing Factors Including Class for Handicapping In North America   37

14. Simple Horse Racing System for Winners Without a Lot of Handicapping ... 40

15. Rating Method for Horses for Handicapping Using Factors of Speed and Class ... 43

16. Horse Racing Probability Calculator For Handicapping and Finding Good Bets ... 46

17. How to Bet On Long Shots and Pick Winners ... 49

18. Some Surprising Ways to Win Horse Racing Bets ... 52

Section 2: 57

1. The Secret Life Of A Horse Player And What It Takes To Win Sometime ... 58

2. A Simple But Powerful Horse Racing Method to Pick Winners and Best Bets ... 62

3. Horse Racing Handicapping the Morning Line and Live Odds For Good Value Bets ... 65

4. Find Horse Racing Information For Handicapping Races ... 68

5. Easy Horse Racing Betting Angles For Profit ... 71

6. Horse Racing Bets, Winning Picks, and Long Shot Methods ... 74

7. A System For Handicapping Horse Races Using Simple Factors ... 77

8. Horse Racing Systems and Handicapping Methods That Work ... 80

9. Two Horse Racing Handicapping Factor Methods   83

10. Free Horse Racing Tips and Suggestions For Picking Winners and Live Horses   86

11. Horse Racing Handicapping Problems and Answers 89

12. Horse Racing System Points and Methods   92

13. Horse Racing Tote Board Systems and Suggestions For Using The Odds To Bet   95

14. Logical Horse Racing Bets and Handicapping Tips With the Favorite   98

15. Horse Racing Handicapping Jockeys and Races   101

16. A Simple Horse Racing System For Easy Handicapping   104

17. Horse Racing Systems and Methods Based On Times   107

18. How To Handicap Horse Races Using The Hierarchy Method   110

Section 3: 113

1. Good Handicapping Method Or System Using Two Horse Racing Factors 114

2 Horse Racing Secrets That Cost You Money 117

3. Using Campaigns to Make Good Bets On Horse Races 120

4. How to Find a Good Horse Racing Bet 123

5. Across the Board Horse Racing Betting Strategy and Best Bets 126

6. Basic Horse Racing Handicapping Steps to Find the Best Bet 129

7. Horse Racing Tips for Cold Weather and Off Tracks 132

8. Are there Any Good Horse Racing Systems 134

9. How to Be Lucky At The Horse Races 137

10. The First Step in Horse Racing Handicapping and Finding Winning Bets 140

11. Horse Racing Bets and Tips That Pay Off 143

12. Quick Handicapping Angles and A Simple and Easy Horse Racing System 146

13. How Important Is Class As A Horse Racing Handicapping Factor 149

14. Horse Racing Winners System Based on Class and Speed   152

15. Horse Racing System Basics to Find Winners and Best Bets   155

16. Horse Racing Betting Strategy for Wheeling Horses 158

17. Find the Best Bet in Horse Racing That Pays the Most for the Smallest Bet   161

18. Easy Horse Racing Handicapping Methods Using Speed   164

Section 4:   167

1. The Key to Horse Racing Betting Strategy For Profits 168

2. Who Wins Money at the Horse Races and How Do They Do It   171

3. A Good Horse Handicapping Method Based on Impact Values   174

4. What Successful Horse Racing Handicappers Look For in a Race   177

5. Horse Racing Handicapping Factors Post Position and Running Style   180

6. Jockey Switches and Handicapping Horse Races   183

7. Handicapping Triple Crown Races For Three Year Olds In N. America   186

8. Using Track Eccentricities to Handicap Horse Races 189

9. Handicapping In The Spring When Tracks Are
"Muddy" Or "Off" 192

10. Horse Racing Handicapping Angles and Tips for Class
and Speed 195

11. Horse Racing Handicapping Using The Best Speed At
the Distance 198

12. Using Trainer Moves Effectively to Pick Horse Racing
Winners   Profitably 201

13. How to Pick Winning Horses by Spotting Big Changes
and Trainer Moves 204

14. Horse Racing Handicapping Angles and the Double
Class Drop 207

15. The Best Way to Win at the Horse Races When Just
Starting Out 210

16. The Double Down or Parlay Bet for Horse Racing 214

17. Horse Racing Speed, Pace, Class, and Distance
Adjustments for Handicapping Angles 217

18. What Are The Best Odds For Horse Racing Bets That
Make a Profit 221

More helpful handicapping books and articles...

Bill Peterson has written full length books that go into depth with many actual examples of the races, including the past performances for each race. Step by step, Bill shows you how to evaluate a race to find the best opportunity for betting success and profit.

In the *Horseplayer Series* Bill starts in ***Horseplayer I, A Winning Strategy***, by evaluating races so you can understand why some favorites win and others lose. In about 70%-80% of the races one of the top 3 horses wins. Bill shows you how to use that to your advantage. Hit more winners and exactas with *Horseplayer I*.

http://www.amazon.com/Horseplayer-Winning-Strategy-Series-Volume/dp/1494936577

In the second book, **Horseplayer II, Longshot Strategy and Angles**, Bill shows you how to find those juicy long shots that are right under everyone's nose! Learn how to manage your money and spread the risk to protect and grow your bankroll. All past performances are included along with explanations of how each long shot was

evaluated and chosen. This is a series of workbooks to teach you how to be a complete and successful horseplayer. Reading these incredible books is like spending a day at the track with one of the most prolific handicappers of our time.
http://www.amazon.com/Longshot-Strategy-Angles-Horseplayer-Peterson/dp/1500913375

To learn more about Bill and to find all his books on the subject of horse racing handicapping, visit his Amazon Author's Page at...
http://www.amazon.com/Bill-Peterson/e/B0044XE19A/

*Though *Horseplayer I* is available on your Kindle, we strongly advise you purchase the paperback version. The full-page, past performances do not show well on the Kindle version. It has received good reviews, but is awkward and difficult for some people to read. Using the paperback version is much easier.

Section 1:

1. Horse Racing Long Shots, Red Flags, and Good Bets

While not all long shots are good bets, many of them deserve a second look while you're handicapping. There's nothing like the thrill of cashing a winning ticket on a long-priced runner, but just blindly betting every horse that goes to post at high odds is financial suicide. Still, many horse players contend that longshots are where the money is to be found. When you handicap, however, do you specifically look for longshots in every race or do you handicap the race, estimate the probability of each runner winning, then determine if any one of the horses that you think is a contender is also at long odds?

If you really want to make money betting on horses then you must learn to determine the probability of a horse winning in order to know if the odds being offered are fair odds. Even though a horse may be at 20-1 and pay $42 to win, it doesn't mean it's a good deal. It would have to win more than one race out of 20 to make it worth betting on and quite frankly, some horses won't win one out of a hundred races.

Are there any signs that a horse is ready to win that are overlooked by the crowd you're betting against? That's the key. As I've said before, horses win for a reason so a longshot with a reason to win is a dangerous horse and may be live. Some of the red flags you should look for when trying to find a long-priced winner are a change in equipment, a new trainer, gelding (the biggest equipment change in racing) and a very fast workout from out of the blue. By that I mean that the horse has been showing mediocre works, but suddenly seems to wake up and post a big figure for a workout.

That's usually an indication that something has happened behind the scenes. It could be that the horse was sick or lame and is now fit and ready. It may also mean that the trainer tried a new tactic or piece of equipment. When a trainer is thinking of adding or taking away blinkers he may try that tactic during a workout and ask the exercise rider to see what he can get out of the horse.

When you handicap a race, even though a horse may not have raced well recently, look for any of the above signs or changes and ask yourself a few simple questions. For instance, "Has this horse won at this distance before?" "Has this horse been working its way back into shape after a long layoff?"

Look for a reason for the horse to win and if there is one, consider betting on that horse unless there is a real solid contender at good odds. On the other hand, be skeptical and don't talk yourself into betting a long shot just because you're greedy. Prepare yourself for long losing streaks as well, if you start backing long shots.

2.
Horse Racing Sight Handicapping For Winners Outside The Box

The past performances are a gold mine of information for handicappers who know how to use them effectively, but when it comes to picking winning horses, those pps are limited. They are strictly about the past and the horse player is trying to figure out what will happen in the very near future. As any good horse player can tell you, there can be a world of difference between then and now.

That's why sight handicapping is so important and can help you to be a much better horse picker and gambler. There's nothing wrong with handicapping by what you see written in a racing form, but after you've read about what the horses have done in the past, shouldn't you find out how they look and feel today when the race will be run?

There are several problems with sight handicapping that keep many people from trying it or mastering it. First of all, it's time consuming. You have to go to where the horses are and look them over. If you handicap the post parade or warm-ups before the race you'll have to spend time looking over the horses rather than chatting with friends or looking over your form.

Another problem, and perhaps this is the one that keeps many people from trying it the most, you have to master it. Picking winners by looking at the horses and assessing their health and fitness is an art, not a science. Many horse players are much more comfortable working with numbers such as speed figures and pace figures. Looking at an animal and trying to figure out if it is fit and healthy is beyond their comfort zone.

While the reasons for not sight handicapping are reasonable when taken in context, they overlook the problem of determining what condition the horse is in just before the race. As living creatures they're susceptible to illness, lameness, nervousness, etc. If you watch the same horse before several races and keep notes you'll know whether it is normal for the horse to sweat and how much sweating is normal. Excessive sweating on one particular day, after you've noted the horse is usually calm in the paddock, can be a warning sign.

It's those types of observations that can save you from a bad bet and that is perhaps the best argument for sight handicapping. You have to know if something is wrong with the runner you plan to back.

3.
Horses Switching Distance May Be a Very Good Bet

Horses are creatures of habit and some of them seem to run better at certain distances, in fact, may be what is sometimes called, "Distance Specialists." When a horse is switching distance from its last race a wise handicapper looks to see if that runner has won at the distance in the past. Sometimes you find that not only has it won at the distance, but it seems to prefer the distance.

For instance, a horse may be switching from a 5 and 1/2 furlong race to a 6 furlong race. Many handicappers will overlook that fact thinking that there is little difference in distance and therefore, little distance in the race. Nothing could be farther from the truth for some horses. If you find that the horse has won several times at 6 furlongs, but, despite having run many 5 and 1/2 furlong races it hasn't won, then you have to factor that into your fair value odds that you set for that horse.

One aspect of the distance preferences of horses that is often overlooked is that they have a running style that may favor the way the course is laid out. For instance, a race starting on a turn, whether a route or a sprint, may favor that early speed horse that gets out good and can hug the rail or cross over to the rail to get the shortest trip.

The plodding type of runner may favor those long grass races because it takes a while to get rolling along and the pace and distance allow it to settle into stride, then gradually gobble up ground until the late stages of the race when it passes the horses that have tired. When placed in a shorter race or a race on a hard dirt surface that favors the early speed horses, this horse may not perform well and never seem to get into the race.

When encountering a horse that is switching distances while handicapping races, always look to see how it has performed in the past at the distance and track. If it hasn't raced at the distance before, don't assume that just because it won at another distance that was similar, such as the example above with the 5 1/2 furlong race and the 6 furlong race, that the horse will adapt well to the new distance.

Look at the running style and layout of the course to find clues as to how it will handle the new distance and race course.

4.
Horse Racing Angles and Suggestions For Better Wagering and More Wins

If you handicap horse races and want to know how to pick more winners and make more money, here are some suggestions based on one good angle. While many people who handicap horse races think about ways to pick more winners and how to handicap the individual horses, few give enough thought to how they should pick a race. With the advent of simulcasting many years ago the horse players of the United States were given the opportunity to pick and choose the races they play.

No longer limited to the races offered by their local venue, horse players can now play a race here and there. Many of them, however, still buy a program and play almost every race on the program. If you want to know how to handicap and make more money, start thinking about the races you play and how easy or difficult it is to pick a winner or isolate a few good contenders. How consistently do the handicappers manage to narrow down the choices so that the winner is found in the top three favorites in the race?

<u>That is a very good gauge of how easy or difficult the race is to handicap</u> and also how often a long shot manages to sneak over the finish line first. There's nothing wrong with betting on long shots, if you can find a good long shot bet. In fact, if you are a player that likes to try to find a horse at high odds that may be live, those races with the inconsistent runners is the place to look.

On the other hand, if you want to use the handicapping factors and rely on them as much as you can, then you need the races where horses run consistently. You learn which ones to play by keeping track of how often one of the three top horses wins. As well as running consistently, another reason that some races are better than others for the serious horse player is that there is some delineation between the top few and the rest of the field.

In races where every horse in the field has a shot at winning it's very hard to narrow it down to a few contenders. The favorites often fail to win in such races and therefore, unless you're specifically looking for a long shot bet, it's better to pass races with huge fields or percentages that show most winners pay in the double digits. This goes against what many handicappers believe and profess, but if the handicapping factors you use to evaluate horses don't work well in that type of race, what chance do you really have of picking a winner?

5.
Trip Handicapping and What to Look For When Watching A Horse Race Replay

Trip handicapping is a good way to spot horses who encounter trouble in a race. That trouble will make them finish worse than they could have if they'd had a better trip and that will make them look worse in the past performances. While handicappers use the past performances to handicap, they'll have little or no idea why the horse seemed to finish so badly. Once in a while some of them will read the race description at the bottom of the charts, but that is rare and the descriptions don't always tell the whole story

So the person who takes the time to watch a race replay will have an edge over the person who doesn't watch it and consequently doesn't know what really happened in the race. Pace and quarter fractions and final results don't tell the whole story. Some handicappers watch a race replay over and over, dissecting each part until they know it all.

What should you look for when you're watching a race replay? Some things are quite obvious. For instance, you might see a rider stand up in the stirrups and pull back on the reins to gather a horse up or avoid a horse that is blocking it. Some horses are so eager they will run up on the heels of another horse. Whatever the case may be, being thrown off stride does take many a horse out of its game and the race is lost right there. This is particularly true in the home stretch and when a horse is advancing along the rail.

Another thing that you will notice, if you practice watching races, is pace matchups. This happens when two horses seem to hook up and run with each other. This is alright if they're just going easily and loping along, but it can be disastrous if a horse uses too much energy trying to match strides with a horse that has more energy at that stage of the race.

If a horse that usually closes or runs off the pace decides to try to keep up with an early speed horse it often makes that horse expend too much energy too fast and tires it out early in the race. Once again, in this situation, the race is lost at that point. Along with pace matchups and being blocked there are other misadventures that can happen in a race. A horse can stumble badly. That often scares horse and rider and they are thrown off their game.

As well as being blocked a horse can be bumped hard or squeezed between horses. I've even seen one horse bitten by another in a race. Anything is possible, but most of the time it goes without comment and therefore only the sight handicappers are aware of the troubled trip and know the horse may race much better with the right trip in today's race.

6.
How To Handicap Horse Racing Workouts and Trainers

Workouts are a good way to evaluate horses, but only if you understand what the trainer was trying to accomplish with the work. In order to understand the meaning of a workout, say a three furlong work in an even 36 seconds, you must also know how fast the track was that day and also how fit the horse was and where it was in its form cycle. For instance, when a horse is in mid-season form you don't have to work it super hard. The purpose of a workout is simply to keep the horse sharp and to get it out of the barn and remind it that it's a race horse. Working such a runner too hard may be counter-productive.

On the other hand, when a horse is being conditioned and is in the early stages of its campaign, it makes more sense to work it harder to condition its muscles and bring it around. That being said, it is still necessary to understand the trainer and his motives because some will train lightly and use races to condition while others demand a horse be in top form before the first race of its campaign. By campaign I mean the start of a string of races, whether the first of the horse's career of merely the start of another racing season for a veteran runner.

The best way to understand workouts is to learn as much as you can about each of the top trainer's habits. Some trainers will train almost every horse the same way while others try to customize a workout routine for the individual runner. A slow workout by one trainer may have great significance and mean that the horse isn't fit, while another trainer may purposely train a horse that is ready to win very slowly so as not to take too much out of that runner before a race.

The only way to know what is going on is to have studied the trainer and to see when he is successful and to look at the workout pattern that led to that success. Keeping notes on the top ten trainers at your local or favorite track is a good idea. While some people don't look at works I think that they are important and if you know the trainer's habits they can be very helpful. If understanding works only keeps you from making one bad bet or leads to a good one, it's still worth it because for many horse players the difference between a good day and a bad day may be that one bet that made the difference between a loss or a profit betting on the horses.

7.
Long Shots, Sure Bets, and Everything In Between

Want to learn how to bet on long shots and win money? The best way to find a live long shot, or at least a race that supports the theory of betting on long shots, is to find a race with a "sure thing." Okay, admittedly, there's no such thing as a sure thing in horse racing, but you'd never know that by the way people wager on some horses. You'd swear that some favorites are just that, a sure thing, and can't lose.

The race itself, not the horses, is where you start to find compelling reasons to bet against the favorite. What kind of a race would shape up well for a false favorite or one that is vulnerable? Any race with a very large field, no matter how bad the other horses look or how good the favorite may appear, is an opportunity to find a horse at high odds <u>with a reason to win</u>.

Just betting all the horses at high odds in

such a race is financial folly, but handicapping isn't about winging it with a horse because it will pay well if it wins, it's about backing a runner that will pay well <u>when</u> it wins -- *big difference there*. So, in most cases, you start with a big field and look over the runners for anything that might signal a change in form or improvement over recent events.

Equipment changes come to mind first of all. The addition of blinkers or taking them off may have a dramatic effect. The horse that has won in the past at the same distance that is now undergoing a change of equipment is always a dangerous horse and must garner some respect. Another possible red flag that should have the long shot players looking closely is first or second time Lasix.

How do you determine that the favorite is vulnerable? Good question. The objective isn't necessarily to find a horse that is certain to lose. It is merely to find a chalk that is bet below fair value odds and therefore a bad bet. Once you establish that the horse taking most of the money in the win pool is a bad bet you will know that some other horse is taking less than its share of action and is therefore a good bet.

You'll suffer long losing streaks if you

choose to play long shots, but in the long run, depending upon how well you evaluate those horses with a reason to win, you may possibly come out ahead. One thing that time has proven is that it is usually better to bet against the crowd than with them. Though favorites win a lot of races, they don't make their backers a profit over the long run. Then why do people bet on favorites? There are people who like the security of knowing that the horse they backed has the best chance of winning, even though they know that in the long run, favorites are lousy bets.

8.
The Top Four Horse Racing Handicapping Factors For Maiden Races

How do you handicap a horse race? Many people compare each horse to the rest of the field, while others look for a single situation that is often called a spot play. Good horse racing spot plays that stand the test of time often get bet down below the fair value odds and therefore become useless as a way to make money betting on horse races.

I recommend good in-depth handicapping in order to estimate each runner's chance of winning and therefore set fair value odds. Once you've established what each horse is worth, the actual odds you can accept at post time and still make a profit, then you may shop for value in the win pool. Those odds, however, may change after the race starts, so one always wants to leave some room for error.

The first and foremost factor to evaluate

the runners in a maiden race must be speed. With the non-winners of a race what you see is what you get (wysiwyg). They usually run greenly, have no idea of how to rate or match up with another horse except to run as far and fast as they can. Therefore, speed is the thing. The actual speed rating in the horse's last race is the most important factor.

The next handicapping factor is class, or breeding in the case of maidens. The breeding of the babies will tell you what to expect, although they may not always run exactly the way their breeding suggests, it is a guide. Using a good guide to sire statistics will help you to determine which horses might have a class or breeding edge.

The stud fee often indicates which sires have been producing the best winners at the highest purse values. Another indicator of class is the level that the trainer starts a young horse racing at. If the conditioner puts his horse in a maiden special weight race he might think he has something special, but if it is entered in a cheap claiming race that may well be the actual level it belongs in.

The third handicapping factor, in my opinion, is the connections. The connections are the owner, trainer, and rider of the horse.

The trainer is by far the most important because he is usually the one who maps out the campaign of the runner and decides when to go for the win after conditioning the horse. Some conditioners are good at winning with horses in the very first race of the horse's career while others need time to get the horse ready mentally and physically. Knowing what the trainer's strengths and habits are can greatly increase the horse player's chances.

Finally, there is form to be considered. In other words, how is the horse running right now and is it rounding into form? Is it getting better with each race and workout? Knowing the form cycle and following it with a young horse is one way to find that winner that has been underestimated by the crowd. While all horses have a form cycle, the cycle is often erratic or interrupted in older horses by injuries or lameness. The younger horse that has a healthier and less abused body will usually round into form more consistently.

9.
What Are The Best Odds To Bet On Thoroughbred Horses

I usually teach would-be handicappers to determine the probability of a horse winning in order to know the fair value odds. In other words, if you know that a horse will win one out of three races and is going to post at four to one odds, it's a good bet. If the same horse with a one in three chance of winning is going to post at even odds, it's a lousy bet.

While I recommend matching the odds to the probability of winning, I also recommend keeping your wagers within a certain range of odds in order to maximize your cash flow and profitability. Why worry about cash flow? Because betting on thoroughbreds is a business, if you're serious about making a profit at the horse races. Even if you only go to the races once or twice a week, if you really work at making your bets pay, it's a part time job. If you haven't been thinking of it in those terms, maybe it's time you did.

You start with a bankroll, a certain amount of money that you have to invest. Like any good business person you have to decide how much you will risk on each part of your business. How big or small will your wagers be on each race and why? Are you betting more on one kind of race than on another kind of race? There may be good reasons for that type of behavior, but knowing why and having a plan is absolutely important or you may blow through your money and never settle into a winning pattern.

Your strike rate means how often you win. You may use sets of ten or twenty bets or any other number you choose. If you win three out of ten, then your strike rate is thirty percent. If you win five out of ten, your strike rate is fifty percent, and so on. The higher your strike rate, the more you may risk on each bet without tapping out and losing it all, but beware of those losing streaks because they do happen. The winner of about 70%-80% of all thoroughbred races in the United States is within the first three favorites. Usually those horses are below 5-1 or somewhere very close to that figure.

I recommend risking your money on horses in the odds range of 5-2 to 9-2 in order to win often enough to keep your bankroll healthy while also making enough profit on each wager to make it worthwhile. You must master handicapping in order to be able to choose one horse from the first three in the odds to bet on. There must be some reason, no matter what it is, that you use to find the best horse. Some use the major handicapping factors and set their own morning line odds. Others use recent form or connections to isolate one horse among the top three.

10.
What Horse Racing Videos Can Teach You and How They Help You To Win

Watching videos of horses as they race can be exciting and also teach you a lot about the horses and the people who ride them. When a new rider comes along I often watch that rider in several races to get an idea of how successful he or she may be. I also determine whether I should be giving him or her any credit in races or simply write that rider off.

Every year a new crop of riders come along. Some of those apprentices will make it into the hall of fame while others will simply fade away, relegated to bush tracks or worse yet, simply to find they can't make it as a professional jockey. After you've handicapped the horses you have to handicap the riders to determine how much they will add or take away from the horse. A good apprentice who still has the bug (weight allowance) can help a horse to win, but a lousy rider, no matter how much weight the horse is carrying, will almost certainly compromise that runner's chances of winning.

Watch a video of a new rider and see how alertly that one gets the horse out of the gate. When running up the backstretch check to see if the jockey gets the horse to settle. This is very important. Look to see if that rider's clearing the saddle or if he or she rides so low that his or her butt is hitting the saddle. Many horses hate that and it will take them out of the race. Even though that's the case, you will still see young riders who get so caught up in the race that they lose the basics they've been taught. They usually don't last long.

As for the horses in the video, once again, you may see something that helps you in the future. For instance, some horses are rail shy and yet they're closers who need to make up ground in the late stages of the race. If one of these horses is starting from an inside post it may not have the courage to go through an opening along the rail and therefore will hold back even though it does have the ability to win the race.

Another thing to look for is a horse that is blocked in a race. If it is blocked and can't win it may go off at better odds in its next race. Follow that horse and evaluate its chances in its next race, factoring in that it was blocked and didn't get to show its true form or speed last time out. Look for signs of ability in races previous to the one with the traffic problems. If it has shown ability, check it in its next race and see if it is better situated to win.

11.
Easy Handicapping Methods Based on the Tote Board Odds

There are a lot of ways to approach the problem of handicapping a horse race and one of them is to understand the odds and what they are showing you when you look at the tote board. Before betting on a horse race, however, just remember that there's no surefire way to make a profit betting on horse races. It's always risky so you should never wager more than you can afford to lose.

While using past performances and understanding the handicapping factors such as speed, class, and form can be very helpful, it's also true that the betting public as a group is quite good at setting odds on the horses at post time that really do reflect the chances of each runner winning the race.

Therefore, when you look at the odds board and see that one horse is at 10-1 while another is at 2-1, it's a safe bet that the 10-1 probably has much less chance of winning the race. That, however doesn't automatically mean that it's not a good bet and in fact, it may be the best bet on the board. In-depth handicapping and a fine understanding of horse racing are the only ways to validate such long shots, however, and that isn't the intention of this article.

My suggestion, if you want an easy method to use strictly for entertainment purposes, is to compare the morning line to the odds board and find horses in the top three betting choices that are also in the top three morning line choices. This overlap between the public's opinion and the handicapper's opinion indicates a horse that is probably an honest betting choice.

Stick with horses in races with short fields of no more than 8 horses and look for value in the top three betting choices. A horse that is in the top three on the odds board, meaning one of the three horses at the lowest odds, that is also in the top three morning line odds and is also in a race with a reasonable number of horses may be a decent bet. Avoid betting the favorite and look to the second and third favorite for more value.

Try to bet as late as possible, when the horses are being loaded into the starting gate if at all possible, because the odds will fluctuate with each click of the computer that keeps track of the money in the pools. You must realize that horse racing betting is arbitrage betting and therefore will change once the race starts and you will not have a chance to change your bet or make another wager. Like I said, it's risky, but with the right system some people do make money.

12.
Guaranteed-Can't Miss- a Bargain at Twice the Price- Horse Racing System For Big Profits and Lower Cholesterol

Does it sound too good to be true that you can actually lower your cholesterol while picking horse racing winner after horse racing winner at incredibly high odds? The title of this article is meant to point out that some people make ridiculous claims for horse racing systems that simply don't work. Then why would you buy such a horse racing system? The fact of the matter is that there are many people who prey on other people who are desperate or simple minded. The truth of the matter is that you have to be realistic in your expectations in life and if something sounds too good to be true, it probably is.

If you're looking to buy a good horse racing system that will help you to pick winners and make money at the race track, let's look at the facts of life and then come up with a picture of what a good horse racing system will look like and what it will actually be able to do for you.

First and foremost, let me be honest with you, I teach people how to handicap horse races. After decades of handicapping horse races I can tell you that it is very difficult to consistently make a profit as a horse player. It is easier to teach other people how to handicap and that's why I do it and why some of the most famous handicappers do it and write those books that may be lining your shelf right now. No one with an automatic system to pick winners that make a profit is going to sell it cheap. In fact, if someone has such a system, they are rich from it and won't sell it at all.

Then why buy a horse racing system? Good question. The answer is that it will teach you some horse racing angles and help you to look at the races from a new perspective. You should expect to learn or gain something from such a purchase, naturally, but don't expect more than a learning experience and to become a better handicapper.

Before you buy, think about what you want from the system and also check to see how reputable the seller is. The first place to look is the guarantee. If there is one it shouldn't have a bunch of catches and it should be straightforward. In other words, if you don't feel that you learned something then you may ask for your money back in a reasonable amount of time. You shouldn't have to prove that you used it, but only that you did buy it and think it didn't deliver what you expected from it.

13.
Horse Racing Factors Including Class for Handicapping In North America

Horse racing itself is pretty much the same the world over. Horses are horses, after all, and so are people, though languages and customs may vary from place to place. One thing that remains the same is that horses love to run against each other and people love to watch them, train them, own them, ride them, and bet on them. Betting, above all else, is what keeps horse racing alive as a sport.

Figuring out which horse(s) to bet on is the tricky part. It comes down to looking at past performances and also looking the runners over on the day they race. Those two methods, when used correctly, can help an astute horse player to determine a horse's chances of winning, in other words, the probability. It isn't an exact science, but when a determined horse player works at it and practices, he or she can often develop the knack for making a pretty good morning line.

When betting on the horses, the morning line should reflect the fair value odds, in other words, a break-even point. The horse player looks for odds above that amount in order to make a profit on all bets. He or she will form an opinion based on how the horses match up for speed, class, form, pace, breeding, connections, and a few other factors, such as recent equipment changes. Each factor is carefully weighed against the others to determine how important each one may be.

Class is perhaps the most difficult to accurately determine. Many modern handicappers use algorithms that compare how well a horse ran in a race to the caliber of the horses it faced. In times past many horse players simply looked at purse values to determine how tough recent races may have been for a runner, but that was not really a good indication of how well the runner handled the challenge of racing at that level. Software and new past performances that show a class rating have improved the use of class as a factor.

The past performances and data files used in North America are perhaps the best or most useful of all because they break down so much information including calls at each stage of the race. Therefore, pace is a factor that can be used with great ease and it's also very useful. Wise handicappers understand that more isn't always more, so they use the best factors to handicap and disregard the rest based on the type of race. Along with actual experience, computer models often point out which factors are the most important.

Therefore, when handicapping today's races a horse player should first consult the overall statistics for the type of race and then compare the most relevant factors.

14.
Simple Horse Racing System for Winners Without a Lot of Handicapping

If you just want an easy way to pick good bets and winners at the horse races there are a few simple systems. Just be warned that making a long term profit from the horse races isn't easy and you will probably want a more advanced horse racing handicapping system for serious long term betting.

Start with the idea that not all the horses in the race have an equal chance of winning. Almost anybody knows that, right? But which horses have the best chance of winning and also paying you enough to make it worthwhile to bet on? It's not usually the favorites because they pay very little and are usually bet way down by the public. At the other end of the scale, while long shots may pay big they also seldom win, hey, that's why they're long shots.

In the middle of the odds, particularly in the horses whose odds are between 3-1 to

9-2, you will often find many good bets. These horses have a chance to win, otherwise they'd be at much higher odds, and yet they pay better than the favorite most of the time. Before you bet on one, however, let's look at a simple system that can narrow down the search.

Horses adding more than a few pounds to the weight they will carry in the race have a poor chance of winning unless every horse in the race is doing the same thing. If, however, there are horses that are in that favorable odds range who are carrying the same weight, they are the better horses to bet from a statistical point of view.

If a top rider gets off a horse in that odds range, never bet it to win. Jockeys are good judges of horseflesh and if a top rider gets off a horse it probably won't win. Eliminate any horse in that odds range that is losing a top jock. Also eliminate any horse in that range with a rider who has less than a 10% winning average. These types of riders are just bad bets.

Horses that finished in the money in a race in the last 39 days are the best to bet on because they've shown that they are in form and though 39 days is stretching it a bit, they may still be in good shape.

Therefore look for a horse that has a competent jockey that stays on, isn't adding more than two pounds, and has finished in the money in the last 39 days. If such a horse is at 7-2 to 9-2 it is often a decent bet. Just remember that this simple horse racing system is meant for fun and if you want to become a serious horse player you will need a more complicated and reliable method.

15.
Rating Method for Horses for Handicapping Using Factors of Speed and Class

Rating horses in order to determine each runner's chances in a race is a good way to find a good bet. The best bets are the ones that have "a positive return on investment expectation." In other words, if you bet this type of horse ten times in a similar situation, you will make enough to cover your wagers with some left over - a profit. While I have simplified this by summing it up, it's actually quite difficult to make a consistent profit betting on horses.

Using several of the most popular and powerful handicapping factors is a good place to start. When you handicap a race, start with speed. Look at each runner's most recent races to see which ones have been running the fastest. Distance does make a difference so look for horses that have done well at the distance or close to the distance, recently.

If there are no horses returning from a long layoff it makes the handicapping job easier. If there are horses returning from extended rests, you must determine if the trainer is capable of bringing a horse back ready to run and if the horse has ever won or raced well after a long layoff.

Start looking for contenders among the three horses with the fastest times in their last race. The winners usually come from the top three in this group about 70% of the time.

Once you've determined who has recent speed look for a class horse. This may not always be one of the top three speed horses, but if it is, that horse may very well go to post as the favorite unless it has a big knock against it. These horses may sometimes also be horses that recently failed as a favorite. If so, there is an excellent chance that it will win the race, especially if the trainer is good at winning with horses that fail as the favorite and race soon after that failure.

See which horses overlap for class and speed and then put them in a hierarchy of the best to worst. Once you've done that you may notice the best horse at very low odds such as 3-5 while one of the others that has a chance to win is at much better odds, say 3-1. That 3-

1 horse may be a good bet. Looking at thousands of races in North America we find that 70%-80% of the winners are from the top three horses in the final odds at post time or in other words, one of the top three betting choices. Look for your best bets among these horses, but shop for value and don't take a ridiculously low price (anything below 2-1).

16.
Horse Racing Probability Calculator For Handicapping and Finding Good Bets

Horse racing handicapping and finding good bets is a difficult endeavor. If you are a good handicapper it doesn't necessarily mean you'll make a profit from your bets as many a good horse player has learned the hard way. Let's see what it takes to not only rate the horses effectively, but to turn that into a profitable experience.

First of all, you do have to learn how to handicap and that means understanding the factors and how they relate to each type of horse and race. The weight you give to the factors of class, speed, connections, and pace will greatly affect how well you do. The only way you'll ever get good at picking winners is to practice. It won't happen overnight.

The probability of a horse winning simply means how likely it is to win. That may be expressed as a percentage or odds. A few simple statistics will help you to begin the process. First of all, about three quarters of the winners of horse races in North America come from the three horses at the lowest odds on the tote board. That means that group of roughly 20%-25% of the horses that go to post win about 75% of the races.

The probability of the favorite, otherwise known as the "chalk," winning varies from race type to race type. Knowing the odds or probability of a favorite winning the race you're handicapping will greatly improve your winning average because you'll know how hard or easy it is to pick the top horse. Since the majority of races are won by the top three you'll be able to figure the probability of the next two horses winning simply by subtracting the percentage of winning favorites from that number.

You may find the probability of the second favorite winning is 25% in some races and much lower in others. Now look at the odds and compare the odds at post time to the actual odds of the second favorite in the race. Do you see how you can begin to look for value? Now combine other factors. Did you know that about 25% of the jockeys win about 75% of the races? At almost any race track there are a handful of jockeys and trainers who win most of the races.

Unless you're specifically looking for long shots with little chance of winning, betting on one of those "other" jockeys is a bad bet. You may be able to estimate probability by multiplying the percentage of winning of the second favorite times the percentage of winning by the top jockey to arrive at a figure.

17.
How to Bet On Long Shots and Pick Winners

It isn't hard to find a long shot to bet on at the horse races. The problem is finding one that really has a chance to win. While any horse in a race has some chance of winning simply because all the others may fall down, there are some runners who have as much chance of winning as a politician passing up a free meal. In other words, it *ain't* gonna' happen.

Yet every day, all over the world, horses do win races and pay a big price. "How often?" you may ask. Well, unfortunately, for most long shot players, not often enough. Most people who play those horses at double digit odds lose consistently and just live for the thrill of cashing the occasional big ticket with no hope of actually coming out ahead at the end of the month. They're adrenaline junkies.

Looking over the charts for races in North America one thing we notice is that most races are won by a horse at less than 5-1. There are long shots in almost every race, but they rarely win. On the other hand, the horses that do win have something going for them that made people bet them down to odds of less than 5-1. Is it possible that there could be something in a long shot's past performances that could be used to signal the horse might win today?

The answer is, "Yes." Before you try to find that red flag that signals a horse is ready to win and pay a big price, however, think about the two horses and how they differ. You have to handicap for those big winners differently than you handicap favorites or you'll never win. Don't use speed ratings or class to find a good bet at high odds because, quite frankly, those horses that do show class and speed won't be at big odds most of the time.

What is it that makes a good long shot bet? It has to have something that is changing today that will make it run faster than it did in the past. Think about that for a moment. If the horse had shown that speed it wouldn't be at those high odds, but without the speed it won't win today, except by some fluke. What will make it faster today and I do mean much faster? Look through your racing program and put a mark beside each high odds horse that has something that may make it run faster today. That's how you start narrowing down the search for a good bet on a horse at high odds.

18.
Some Surprising Ways to Win Horse Racing Bets

Do you sometimes wonder if you can ever win? There is a bet that could probably help you to make money, but it isn't the bet that you may think it is. It may or may not be the win bet, though the best bet in horse racing is the straight win bet. That wager requires only one horse and in most places it has the lowest take out compared to other bets. While there are some gimmick bets such as pick fours and pick fives that offer lower takeouts, the chances of hitting one of those pick fours or pick fives is pretty low unless you play many combinations. When it comes to a win bet, there's only one horse and one bet you have to make.

There's another bet that can make you money and this is the one bet you'd never guess because it's the bet you never make. Make a list of your bets for the day and rate them from the ones you feel the most confident about to the ones that are the shakiest. Then, just drop the bottom third, in other words, the ones you have the least confidence in.

You've probably just saved yourself some money. Horse players think of their betting in terms of a campaign or set of wagers. For instance, while you may look at your last wager or day at the races and think of it as a win or loss, the horse player who is in for the long haul may look at a week, month, or even a whole meet and only call it a win or loss when he is done playing. The same is true of sets. He may play a set of twenty races and only then consider whether he's won or loss.

Here's a winning angle, a way to improve your wagering and handicapping. If you look at your last twenty bets and then weed out a quarter or a third of them, would you have made more money? Nine out of ten horse players would say, "yes. If I hadn't made those bets I'd have lost less and might even be ahead."

Therefore, if you count your next twenty bets and instead of making all twenty, you drop five or six that you consider a bit dodgy, you may find the bets you don't make will turn your losing ways into a profitable campaign.

It isn't always the wagers we make that make a profit for us, it's also the wagers we don't make that we could have made. Learn to weed out a bad bet here and there and you may start to have more good days and fewer losing days.

Section 2:

1.
The Secret Life Of A Horse Player And What It Takes To Win Sometimes

If you aspire to be a horse player or you're a weekend warrior and just play the horses on weekends and when you can, here's a look at how this horse player lives to give you a glimpse at the not so glamorous life of a guy who handicaps horse races and tries to make it pay. You'll notice that I added that word, "sometimes," to the title of the article.

That's because right off the bat I'd like you to know that gambling, and that's what betting on horses is, is an up and down existence and a regular roller coaster financially and emotionally. I'm not complaining because I did choose the life and sometimes I do quite well, but like most people I've created a bad situation in my life and now I'm making the best of it. Playing the horses isn't the bad part, having a regular life with a family and relationships and all the rest is what complicates it.

Having a family isn't bad, but if you're going to really apply yourself to beating the races, prepare yourself to be letting someone down at some point in your life because you won't be there for them. For instance, on this morning it's five o'clock AM and I'm crawling out of a nice warm bed and there is someone in it who would prefer to have me stay with her. It's her day off and she'd like to snuggle up to me and sleep a few more hours, but I'm driven to get out of bed and go to work. She has a regular job with a paycheck and benefits and one of the benefits that is not lost on me is that she gets to roll over and go back to sleep while I head for the coffee maker and my office in my slippers.

Work is turning on the computer and looking over my notes and the past performances and race summaries and trying to start to plan my campaign for the day based on what has worked in the past and what hasn't. That changes, though, and I have to be careful to keep an eye on the trends and track biases. I look at race summaries for an hour and do some pace handicapping. I write some notes on a few horses that will go off at decent odds and that have a pace advantage in their races.

Then I get into the actual past performances to look at a few angles I've been checking out lately. I notice a few horses that fit the profiles I'm looking for and make a note of them. I estimate their fair value odds and write them beside them in the programs I've printed out. Printing out the programs is expensive and time consuming and I'm filling the landfill with old racing programs and I feel guilty about all the trees that get cut down, but quite frankly, being a bit of a dinosaur whose been playing the races for decades, I need a written program in my hand to look at and make notes on. In fact, there are stacks of such programs all over my tiny office so it isn't exactly a landfill that's getting filled, although certain persons who live with me have made the comparison between my office and the local dump.

But enough about that, what's the secret that I mentioned? There's nothing secretive about getting up in the morning and going to work, even if you do it in your slippers. The secret is that I love what I'm doing and if you are trying to beat the races and don't wake up in the morning excited about the challenge, you'd better forget it. Horse racing handicapping has been called an intellectual sport, sort of like chess, and if you don't absolutely love it and the challenge it presents, you'll never make it.

2.
A Simple But Powerful Horse Racing Method to Pick Winners and Best Bets

There are many ways to pick horses to bet on and many handicapping systems that work some of the time, too. While nothing works all the time one thing is very clear, if you don't use some kind of handicapping or picking method, your random choices will have random and disappointing results. If that sounds familiar, here's a little advice.

If you don't like handicapping with numbers or figures and if pace handicapping isn't your idea of a good time there is another way to make good bets and possibly a profit, though it's wicked hard to do at the horse races. Try being a horse racing handicapping detective. No, I'm not crazy. Here's what I mean.

You'll have to have access to the horse races and you'll have to be patient and enjoy watching the horses and people. Just look at it this way, the more you know about those beautiful animals and the people who race them, the better your chances of making money. Start by observing them in the paddock and saddling ring. Keep notes about the horses. Obviously you can't follow all the horses on a card, but you can choose a reasonable number of them to watch and follow so that after a while you will have some good reasons to go to the races and enough horses to watch to keep you occupied all day.

Make notes about their equipment and the jockey and trainer. Make a special note of any horse wearing a tongue tie or a nasal strip for the first time. They sometimes make a big difference and the public is usually unaware of them. Be meticulous in your observations of the horses and people. Is the horse sweating and if so, how much? Too much sweating is a bad sign.

Is the jockey excited or at least awake? Does he or she seem to want to ride the horse or is that rider bored and expecting a loss? Is the trainer smiling and happy, possibly expecting a win? These conditions will change from week to week and your notebook full of notes about the horses will start to pay off as you see the ones that are improving and those that are not improving and may even be declining.

None of this requires crunching numbers

or sitting in front of a computer or poring over a racing form. On the other hand, it can produce winners that people who rely on a computer or form may miss. Think about it. It's a different kind of handicapping that very few people try.

3.
Horse Racing Handicapping the Morning Line and Live Odds For Good Value Bets

If you're handicapping horse races and trying to determine the odds that are right for the runners you may be tempted to use the morning line. Many people wonder which is more accurate, the morning line or the actual odds shown on the tote board? My experience has led me to go with the tote board as the most reliable indicator of actual probability even though the odds do not always accurately reflect the actual chances of a horse winning.

The difference between the live odds and the probability of a horse winning offers opportunity for a bettor, but first you have to know how to determine that probability and apply it to the price you'll receive based on the tote board at post time. There is also the nasty problem of the prices changing after the race starts and the tote computer doing its final calculations. To say that betting on horse races is risky is an understatement and yet, many people do bet on them.

The trend seems to be that favorites are

often bet down below their actual expectancy and so are long shots. These two groups seem to be the most attractive to most of the betting public. One group is looking for the security of betting the supposed best horse in the race, i.e., the favorite and the other group is looking for a big score with a long shot, never realizing that though the odds are long on them the actual probability of most of them is even worse than those odds indicate so they're a bad bargain, too.

If you consider that the takeout, or "vig," as it is often called, is around 15%-19% and deduct that from the pool and your investing dollars, you'll find that you must recoup that amount before any profit is made on your wagers. Somewhere among the runners, however, there may be one that is offering a price that is close to an even proposition because the public has wagered more heavily on the other horses.

Knowing that the favorite and long shots are bet down below fair value we must look somewhere in the middle range for most of the good bets that will come along at the horse races. Statistically the first three favorites win about 75% of the races. Knowing that the favorite is almost always a bad bargain, the next two favorites are the logical place to look for value. If the favorite wins about 33% of the time and the top three favorites win 75% that means that the other two favorites must win about 42% of the time.

That high average combined with the possibility of a value bet makes those two horses the first choice in our search for value bets.

4.
Find Horse Racing Information For Handicapping Races

We live in the information age, but sometimes it's still difficult to handicap a horse race successfully because some important piece of information is unavailable or hard to find. While there's a wealth of data and statistics out there, it's often the other stuff that I call incidental or peripheral, that matters. I mean the human element and the stuff that goes on behind the scenes.

Sometimes you have to be in the right place at the right time to see something that most of the rest of the people who bet on the race miss. I once saw a jockey at Tampa Bay Downs give a quick signal to someone standing at the fence at the paddock. I may have been the only person who saw the rider quickly raise three fingers in such a way that his body shielded the movement from all but a few of us. Yes, the three did win the race at respectable odds, too.

Depending upon such serendipitous events to make a profit at the races is crazy, but keeping one's eyes open and paying attention isn't. Positioning yourself near the saddling ring and watching the people as well as the animals isn't a bad idea, too, because their body language and bits of conversation you may pick up may help you to have a winner or two or even to avoid a bad bet.

Watching online forums is another way to pick up on the scuttlebutt that goes around the horse racing world. Finding out that a jockey has been sick with the flu all week but is still riding his mounts is a good bit of info to have. Or learning that another rider is having personal problems that may be affecting his riding can help you to decide if you really want to back his mounts.

Yes, the most important part of handicapping races is using the factors in the past performances to rate each horse in the race and to compare them to one another, but since humans play such an important part in the game, you must be aware of what is going on with them.

Another source of sometimes overlooked material is the comments section of the charts and also the workouts. Too many people disregard workouts and workout patterns simply because they don't understand them. Clocker's notes are of utmost importance and yet you rarely see a public handicapper referring to them when giving his or her rundown of the race. Learn to read the opinions of others when those others do know what they're talking about. You'll be ahead of the game and pick some nice winners.

5.
Easy Horse Racing Betting Angles For Profit

Betting on horse races and finding good bets that show a profit over a long period of time is very difficult. If you want to make money on horse races you'll probably have to work very hard, but there are a few angles that may pay off quickly if you hit them at the right time. A little luck and the right bets can sometimes make for a nice day at the races.

One exacta betting angle that has brought home some nice long shots is to bottom wheel the favorite or second favorite in any race with a field of ten horses or more. The idea behind this angle is that there are so many horses in the race that at least one of them is going to beat the favorite. The bigger the field, the better the odds that an outsider will win. Big fields often produce big exacta payoffs. Even when the favorite or second favorite is the second horse in the exacta the payoff can be in the triple digits.

Another good betting angle is to bet on any maiden that has one of the top three speed ratings in its last race and is going to post at 5-1 or higher. The winner of many maiden races can be found in the top three speed horses and yet, since so much money is wagered on the favorite, the other speedy horses that have shown some talent are often overlooked. You must, however, get at least 5-1 odds.

Bullet works and equipment change combinations are often good bets. The horse that shows a bullet workout and also has an equipment change such as an addition of blinkers or Lasix is often a winner. The reason is that the trainer has just tried the change of equipment in a workout to see if it would make a difference and it has.

One of the problems with handicapping horses that have an equipment change is that you often just don't know if it will make the horse faster. In the case of the horse that has the equipment change and a bullet, you can see that the horse has improved. Naturally, betting on horse races is risky and these angles should be used for entertainment purposes only. If you're going to bet real money on a horse race I suggest using a good system and learning how to handicap properly. On the other hand, if you just want some fun and easy to find bets, these will fill the bill.

6.
Horse Racing Bets, Winning Picks, and Long Shot Methods

Finding good horse racing picks for free and picking good bets at the horse races is not easy, but it is possible. The first thing to look for in a good horse racing pick is whether or not it will pay well enough to offset your losses. The way this is done is to estimate the probability of the horse winning in other words, to determine how many times it would win in ten or twenty races.

For instance, a horse that would win three races out of ten would have a 30% probability of winning. Based on two dollar win bets it would cost you $20 to bet the horse ten times and you would therefore need it to pay at least $7 each time it won to make a dollar profit. (3x7=$21) Therefore, the whole secret to making money at the horse races is to find bets that outperform the crowd's expectations.

The reason for that is that the public's opinion of a horse's chances is expressed in the odds on the tote board. They will bet it down to the odds that they think it should be at to win. No, they don't all get together and work it out, but that happens naturally in a self regulated market, as the horse racing betting pools are sometimes described. It simply means that enough people will think the horse has some chance to win and will wager on it. The more who think it will win the lower the odds.

If the horse is under-bet then there's an opportunity to make some profit as pointed out above. The good horse player or handicapper must be able to determine how likely a horse is to win based on handicapping factors. If the handicapper thinks a horse should have a one out of three chance to win, but the horse will pay 4-1 odds, it's considered a good bet.

Straight win bets offer the best opportunity to compare the actual payoff with the probability of winning and therefore many handicappers set their own morning line odds. Consider this when determining your own probability. Horses that are adding more than two pounds from the weight they competed at last time out have a much smaller chance of winning than horses that are not adding more than two pounds.

Horses moving up in class have much less chance of winning. Also, and here is one of the most important stats, horses in the top three favorites have about a 75% chance of winning. Looking for a value bet in the top three contenders is most likely to pay off often enough to make it worthwhile.

There are good long shot bets, but they're hard to spot without a good horse racing handicapping system.

7.
A System For Handicapping Horse Races Using Simple Factors

Sometimes horse racing handicapping systems are very complicated, while other systems are simple. Naturally, the more work you put into finding good bets the more likely it is that you'll make money at the horse races. On the other hand, sometimes the best answer to a difficult problem is the simple answer. It's possible to make the problem of finding the best horse at the best odds too complicated.

As they say, "Over analysis leads to paralysis."

You may make it so complicated that you finally can't decide which horse is the best. That may be for one of several reasons. Perhaps the horses are so evenly matched that it's hard to separate them according to ability or maybe while each one has some positive attributes you've confused yourself by looking at each factor as being equally important.

The simple factors that you would use to

handicap may be speed ratings, jockey win ratings, class, and pace. Of course, recent success is a powerful factor that can't be over looked because it indicates recent form. If a horse just raced well and isn't moving up in class or adding more than a few pounds in weight, it has to be considered.

A handful of jockeys usually win the majority of races at a track so look at the win percentages of each rider. Any good rider with a horse that has a speed rating in the top three for last race or that has one of the highest average speed ratings has to be considered a contender. Good bets are often found when you find a horse with a competent rider and some back speed.

Back speed means that in the past the horse was fast at the distance, but may have thrown in a few clunkers lately. That horse has shown it has the ability, so it has class at that level, but may have been lame or sick for a while. A good trainer and a good rider will often manage to get another good race out of the horse.

So look for a good jockey and a horse that has shown some speed at about the same distance and class level. Don't be afraid to bet against the favorite. They only win about a third of the time. As long as your pick is getting some action on the board and isn't a big time long shot, take the good odds. In the long run that's what you need to make money betting on horse races. Just remember, it's risky and never bet more than you can afford to lose.

8.
Horse Racing Systems and Handicapping Methods That Work

Let's start by being realistic and acknowledging that making a profit betting on horses, even with a very good handicapping method, is difficult and very risky. The best handicappers have a hard time maintaining a consistent profit and the life of a horse player is full of ups and downs. Therefore, though you may make money betting on horses, be prepared for many wins and losses and the strain of uncertainty.

There are systems that do sometimes work for picking winners and the best of them also look for value. That's the hardest part of being a good horse player - finding value. It's all based on the actual probability of the horse winning compared to the actual odds on the tote board. The problem, as many of you have found, is that the odds change after the race starts and a horse that offered odds of 2-1 may drop far below that level. If you're basing your wagering decision on the tote board odds you'd better have a good margin to work with.

Once again, let's be realistic. While you can find good systems that point out good horse racing angles and will help you to become a successful horse player, no system that you buy straight off the shelf is going to make you rich and remember, you heard that from a man who teaches people how to handicap.

Any horse racing system that is worth its salt will help you to find a good horse to bet on and will also work some of the time, but as I often tell folks, while anything works some of the time, nothing works all the time. The good horse player learns when to use each of the systems he has learned to pick winners or winning exotic bets such as exactas and trifectas or even multi-race bets such as the pick 3 or pick 4.

If you're serious about learning how to handicap and don't want to waste your time or money, then don't buy a product that makes unrealistic claims such as making you rich over night or picking an unrealistic percentage or number of winners. You also want to avoid anything that tells you that you can play every race. No horse player, no matter how good, can play every race and come out ahead.

In fact, another factor that many systems have is to teach which races to bet on and which ones to avoid.

9.
Two Horse Racing Handicapping Factor Methods

When you learn how to handicap horse races it usually involves what are known as handicapping factors. Here's a brief look at the major factors and some methods for using them. First of all, since it is racing, we'll look at speed. Speed ratings are more useful than the actual times it took to run the races in the horse's past performances. That's because all race tracks aren't the same and some play much faster than others. Not only that, but the times vary from day to day. So always use the speed figures rather than the actual times that the horses posted.

Probably the most reliable figure is the one from the last race as long as the horse got around cleanly with no mishaps or traffic problems. Start your speed handicapping by looking at the last speed figure and then look at the average for the last three races. The horse that has the highest speed rating at the distance should also be noted. If that horse appears to be in "form," it will probably be the favorite, though sometimes it will be a second favorite. It's hard to beat speed, but it's also usually over bet so look for a horse that is almost as fast, but offers better value.

Another important handicapping factor is class. This is perhaps the most arbitrary and difficult of all methods, but it has to be taken into consideration. How you measure class is the problem and there is no one right way. Some believe the purse value of the races that a horse has raced in denote that horse's class. On the other hand, some handicappers argue that purse values alone don't tell the whole story.

They contend that class is measured by the actual success the runner had against the quality of horses it faced. For instance, if one horse managed to run second in a $20,000 claiming race and another horse ran 6th in a $35,000 claiming race, which one is the classiest? What if they are both in a $15,000 claiming race today? As you can see, it's a thorny issue and you have to develop some method for comparing class consistently.

I think the method of comparing actual success to the quality of the horses is best, though certainly not perfect. It's definitely not an exact science, but if you also factor in pace, you may be able to arrive at some idea of how the horse will handle the pace and class today. Like all handicapping factors, class alone is not enough to form a clear opinion about a horse.

When used together, however, both class and speed often do point out a horse with a significant edge over the field.

10.
Free Horse Racing Tips and Suggestions For Picking Winners and Live Horses

Finding a good bet or a live horse, as they are sometimes called, isn't easy, but it can be done. The best way to approach horse racing betting is as a hobby and an expensive one, too, if you don't get it right. Therefore, the first tip is, "Don't bet the farm." The second tip is to always find value before you bet. Odds of less than 2-1 rarely pay off in the long run.

So as you bet, while your first concern may be to find the most likely winner, your second goal should be to find the horse at the highest odds that really does have a chance to win. If a horse won its last race it may very well be the favorite in today's race. If nothing is changing with the horse, such as the weight carried, jockey, distance, class, etc., then it may be the most likely horse as far as its chances of winning.

If it is bet done below our 2-1 mark, however, you may wish to look for another horse that has a chance and yet is at higher odds than the favorite. A good tip is, "Don't look deeper in the field than you have to." In other words, the most likely horses are usually at the lowest odds. While it may be thrilling to cash a ticket on a long shot, it doesn't happen often, so stick with horses at lower odds and you'll cash many more tickets. Plus, it's more fun to win many times rather than once in a while, like most long shot bettors do.

Once you've gotten past the favorite, if it won its last race as in the example above, look for horses that are changing something today. For instance, if the horse is adding blinkers or Lasix or if a top jockey is now getting on the horse. Why look for changes? Because changes are how horses improve. The trainers keep trying different things, including conditioning the horse with workouts and races, until they find the key and win.

Doing the same thing over and over again and expecting different results is insane. Betting on the same horse that is running with the same equipment and rider in the same class of race and expecting different results is insane, so look for the horse with a new trainer or rider or some other change. If it is at high enough odds to be worth a bet and yet low enough to suggest the public has some faith in it, it may be a good bet.

11.
Horse Racing Handicapping Problems and Answers

When it comes to handicapping horse races and picking winners, there are no rules that apply all the time. When it comes to betting on horses or anything else for that matter, there is one formula or rule or method, call it what you will, that must be followed to make a profit. I'm writing about the ratio of risk to reward. In other words, the probability of the horse winning must outweigh the risk. Here's how you figure that out.

Start by handicapping the race using the basic handicapping factors, if you know how to do it. If not, start with some other way of rating the horses so that you can determine a hierarchy of the best to the worst in terms of ability. Obviously the likelihood of a horse winning a race, otherwise known as probability, has a direct effect on the probability of it winning. The next problem, and this is the toughest one when it comes to making money betting on horses, is to figure out how many times the horse would win the race if it was run ten times with exactly the same runners and conditions.

That's the biggest problem handicappers face and there are no easy answers or solutions, though it is possible to arrive at a reasonable guess. If you have a hierarchy of horses formed either by the morning line (not too reliable) or the odds at post time (more reliable, but not perfect) start with the favorite or most likely to win. This may actually vary, but you have to use some figure even if you can't really accurately determine that percentage of times the horse would win.

A reasonable figure for the top horse is 2-1 since most favorites win about a third of the time. A horse at 2-1 will pay $6 for every $2 bet, so if you bet it three times and it wins once you've spent $6 and received $6. That makes 2-1 a break-even point for many favorites and top betting choices. So if you can't compute the odds that you think the favorite should be at, use 2-1. Set the second favorite at 3-1 and the third favorite at 4-1. Look for the horse in the hierarchy that is going to post at higher odds than you have allowed according to its place in the hierarchy.

Sticking with the top three horses is a good idea since the winner of most races is found in the top three betting favorites. While this is a simplistic system for rating bets and horses it does help with one of the problems of rating them. As you gain experience as a handicapper you will be able to adjust these figures accordingly.

12.
Horse Racing System Points and Methods

There are many ways to pick winners and evaluate horses before a race. Some call them systems while others say they are a method to pick winning horses. Whatever the case may be, they all rely on points that relate to horse racing handicapping factors. The major factors of class, speed, pace, form, and connections are easier to evaluate if you use a points system.

For instance, when looking at speed as one indicator of ability it may be helpful to also look at these three points. First of all speed in last race is probably the most reliable indication of form if the race was within a reasonable amount of time. Using 30 days may be a little too restrictive, but going over 40 days is too lenient. I think the best way to approach the problem is to look at the horse that has posted the best speed rating in the last 36 days or less.

While the best speed is important, so is consistency and another way to use the speed handicapping factor is to look at average speed at the distance. That may work with older horses that have had enough races at the distance to average those figures out. A minimum of three races is best when using averages. On the other hand, how far back shall we look? If the horse is 7 or 8 years old and scored its highest speed ratings as a 4 year old, the most recent speed ratings are probably a much better indication of its current form and ability. That's a decision the handicapper needs to make and there's no rule that would apply to all situations. It's important to be consistent in comparing the runners in order to properly compare each one to the field in the race.

The same is true of all the factors. Be consistent. When it comes to a class handicapping method, you may use the amount of money earned per race as one way to find true class or you may simply look at the purses in recent races. If you do use purse value as a class handicapping method I advise you to also look at how well the horse actually ran in those races. It's not enough to run in a classy race, the horse must have also shown that it really fit with those runners as well. A rough rule of thumb is whether the horse finished within five lengths of the winner or managed to finish in the money. If it fits either of those conditions, it may have belonged in that class.

Whatever handicapping system or method you use always be consistent and look for value when you bet. Just because a horse has more ability, it doesn't mean it's a better bet.

13.
Horse Racing Tote Board Systems and Suggestions For Using The Odds To Bet

The odds board tells a lot about the horses and each runner's chance of winning in a horse race if you know how to use it. First of all, as almost everyone knows, when looking at the odds in North America, the favorite or horse at the lowest odds wins about a third of the time. Like I said, almost anyone knows that, but if you didn't, now you do. How can that information help you?

From race to race, because there are different kinds of race types, the favorite may not necessarily have a one out of three chance of winning. Looking closer at the odds, how close is the next favorite in the betting choice and how low are the odds? Let's say that one horse, the favorite in this case, is at 6-5.

The next betting choice is at 8-5. While it's true that the favorite has a great chance of winning, the horse at 8-5 has a very good chance as well. The actual odds on the tote board, while not perfect, are often a very good indication of a horse's true chances of winning. If there are only one or two horses at very low odds, let's say less than 4-1, then they have an excellent chance of winning and one or both may be a good proposition. It may even be possible to Dutch them and make money.

It's important to remember, however, that the odds are the odds to win, not to place or show and there may be one or more horses that are excellent place bets or second horses in the exactas. In the case above, with two horses at less than 2-1, it may be that they are the best horses to key on for the top spot in the exacta, but when it comes to the second spot, you may want to go much deeper in the odds.

For instance, if there are some live horses in the odds range below 10-1, they may very well have a good chance to place, though they are poor win bet propositions. In the case above it may pay to key those two big time horses over anything under 10-1 in the race. Just boxing two favorites, such as the two horses at 6-5 and 8-5, is rarely a good bet because when punters see such low odds many of them immediately box those two and drive the prices down below fair value.

14.
Logical Horse Racing Bets and Handicapping Tips With the Favorite

While things that work at the races, the angles and tips, aren't always a logical choice, there are some things that you can do and bets you can make that are very logical. Here are a few tips. First of all, it's logical to bet the favorite in a race, but not necessarily to win. The favorites do win more races than any other betting choices. If you key on the favorite in every race your key horse will win about a third of the time and finish in the exacta about half the time while being in the money about three quarters of the time.

If you play that one with the right horses in exotics and you may eke out a profit. The key to it all, of course, is which horse to put with the favorite in order to make a profit? While identifying the favorite, or chalk, is easy (it's the horse with the lowest odds), identifying the horse or horses to play with that one to round out your wager is the tricky part.

Here are a few handicapping suggestions that will require a little work, but will also pay well enough in exotics to give you some chance to make a profit. First of all, playing the favorite and second favorite in an exacta may actually hit many winning tickets, but because they are usually the crowd's first choice, and consequently the lowest paying exacta, they just don't usually make a profit in the long run. So let's throw the second favorite out of our combinations.

When keying the favorite on top I advise that you go deep enough in the betting choices to make it pay at least 5-1. Therefore, look at what the exacta with the favorite over the third favorite is paying and only play if the exacta pays at least 5-1. That means at least a $12 payoff with the chalk on top.

Statistically, the chalk wins more than it places. If it wins about 33% of the time, but is only in the exacta about 50% of the time, well, you do the math. It doesn't appear that the chalk is a very good bet in the bottom of the exacta so why not throw it out? If it wins you want it over a horse at a bit of a price and since it isn't much of a place proposition, because it will still be bet down, throw it out once you've used it on top.

15.
Horse Racing Handicapping Jockeys and Races

One method that is often over looked when it comes to handicapping horse races is to follow a jockey and to really get to know a lot about that rider. Jockeys are superb athletes and there's quite a bit of information available about them if you're willing to dig. Just following one rider for a few weeks you can get to know a lot about that one.

For instance, you can learn which trainers he wins for and also whether that trainer is hot or not winning many races. Another good piece of handicapping information is how well the rider does from different post positions. Much is written about how horses handle different posts and which posts have an advantage, but little is ever mentioned about the rider's who make decisions about which paths to follow.

While a rider may not get to choose the post position the horse starts from, that rider may have reasons to perform better or worse depending on how he likes the post. For instance, some riders don't like being on the rail and feel boxed in. While a professional may still do his best to win the race, if he is uncomfortable or frightened on the rail, that will be picked up by the horse and the horse may not race well.

The same is true of a horse that is in tight in a long race that starts on a turn. Some route races where the starting gate is close to the turn put a rider in an awkward position if he is mid-pack with a runner that is only moderately fast out of the gate. You will often see such runners strung out wide on the turn. Sometimes they also get in tight, almost running up on another horse or getting bumped repeatedly.

Traffic problems can lead to a spill and riders try to avoid such situations. Younger riders have a tendency to be more daring, perhaps because they haven't spent as much time in the hospital as the older riders. So it's good to follow a rider to watch and learn his style and strengths and weaknesses so that when he rides you'll have some idea of how he'll handle the post and horse's running style.

Look at it this way, if you can eliminate one or two races that a top jockey has in the course of a day, that will make his wins that much more profitable for you. Knowing which rides will be problematical for him will help you to lay off some horses even if the crowd is all over them because there's a good jockey up in the irons.

16.
A Simple Horse Racing System For Easy Handicapping

There are ways to quickly handicap horse races and easy horse racing systems you can use that will help you to find good horseracing bets. Naturally, the more time and effort you put into evaluating the runners in a race the better your chances of making money betting on horse races, but sometimes you can actually over-analyze a race and as they say, "Over analysis leads to paralysis." In other words if you look at a race too long you'll eventually become so confused that you won't be able to make a decision or have an opinion about the race.

So sometimes, as they say, "Less is more." Use this simple method to compare the runners in a horse race and to find a good bet. By good bet I mean one that pays more than the horse is worth. If a horse has a one out of three chance of winning, a break even bet would be at 2-1 which would pay $6 for every

$2 wagered.

If you had bet the horse three times and won once you'd spend $6 and get $6. If, however, after handicapping the race and evaluating the runners you see that horse at 4-1 at post time, you know it's a profitable bet. Find enough such bets and you'll make money betting horse races. However, these situations don't occur in every race so you'll have to sit some out.

A simple handicapping method is to average each horse's speed in the last three races or at the distance. It's easier with older horses because they've had more races and their speed and ability are pretty apparent. You can use speed or any other handicapping factor to determine the best horse(s) in the race.

Once you've determined each horse's ability based on speed or any other handicapping factor you choose, place them in order using the Ladder Handicapping System or any other method that will arrange them in a hierarchy. Next, at two minutes to post time write the odds beside each horse from the tote board.

You will quickly see that some horses are over-valued and others are under-valued. Your best plays will usually be found in the second or third favorite. The top three favorites win about three quarters of all races so putting most of your time, effort, and money into one of the top three betting choices makes good sense. This is an incredibly simplistic look at a very complicated subject and meant as an example to help you to start thinking in terms of value. For more detailed handicapping help, read the *Horseplayer Series* of books.

17.
Horse Racing Systems and Methods Based On Times

Since the advent of speed ratings and adjustments made with variants many people have stopped handicapping using time as a factor. By that I mean the actual time it took to run the race as well as the fractional times. But just because we have adjusted times to use now, don't think that scanning those actual times isn't a useful handicapping tool and can't be used as part of a system or method of evaluating the horses.

If you know what the par time is for a particular distance at your local track, scanning those times in a horse's lines can quickly help you to spot a horse with a superior time. Another great use for this is to look at the fractional times and to spot a horse that turned in a very fast fraction. There are several methods to use that information.

For instance, let's say you scan the quarter times for a horse and see it usually goes the first quarter in a time between 23 and 24 seconds, but then see one race where it went a flat 22, say in its last race. You know that was abnormally fast and probably took away any chance that the runner had to finish well at the end of the race. While you may have your own systematic way of handicapping races, adding a quick look at times can be very helpful and shouldn't be discounted as a means to handicap.

Another thing this will often help you to spot is a horse that lays over the others whether it be in final time or pace (whether early or late). Spotting a stand out horse is very helpful and of course, all other handicapping factors should still be considered before making a final selection. Remember, that though a horse may have an edge, it may still not be a good bet if the odds of winning (payoff) are less than the probability of winning.

Some systems actually compare final times or speeds to the odds being offered in a race. For instance, if you average each horse's speed and then put them in a hierarchy from the best to the worst, then compare that hierarchy to the actual odds on the tote board, you can sometimes find a horse that is under bet compared to its ability, that's one very good way to find a good bet. Average speed compared to odds is just one way to find overlays and underlays.

18.
How To Handicap Horse Races Using The Hierarchy Method

There are many ways to handicap a horse race to find the best horse and some good bets. Though handicapping is just a way to look at the runners to decide how they compare to each other, the final goal is actually to compare bets. The odds are what matter in the end because no matter how good a horse may be, if the odds aren't right, it's a bad bet.

How can that be? Because no matter how good a horse may be there's always the chance that it may lose the race. Some people think that they're trying to pick a winner and that it's a one step process, but it's not if you want to make money betting on horse races.

First you determine the probability and then you compare the probability to the odds to determine if the horse is really worth a bet. For instance, if a horse has a fifty-fifty, or even chance of winning, it will win one out of two races. If it goes off at 3-5 odds it will pay $3.20 when it wins. A horse with an even chance of winning is a very good horse. Most horses have far less chance of winning. But, is it a good bet at 3-5? No.

If you wager $2 on two races to collect once and get $3.20 you will lose $.80 for every two races you play. That's why you compare the odds to probability. Using the hierarchy method you start by evaluating each horse and making an estimate of how likely it is to win, in other words, the probability of that one winning. Then place them in a column with the best horse on top and then, in descending order according to probability, each horse in the race.

Then put the odds beside each one that is your best guess or estimate of its actual chance of winning. A very good horse might be at quite low odds, say, 2-1. That means it will have to pay at least $6 for you to break even. Put the odds of probability beside each runner and then wait until post time or as close as you can get without being shut out. Put the odds from the tote board beside each horse and compare them to the odds of probability that you calculated.

Find the horse that is closest to the top that is going off at longer odds than the odds of probability. That's your best bet. This method takes practice, but after a while, if you stick with it, you'll develop the skill of handicapping so that you can spot a good bet when you see one. If there's no profitable bet, skip the race and remember, it's always risky betting on horse races so never risk more than you can afford to lose.

Section 3:

1.
Good Handicapping Method Or System Using Two Horse Racing Factors

There are many ways to handicap a horse race. This method uses just two factors, speed and class, probably the two most important factors. Of course, everything is relative when it comes to evaluating horses in a race. For instance, if a horse hasn't raced for a year, the figures you're using are old and pretty useless, so some common sense is required. If there are such horses in a race you must make the decision of whether or not you have a strong enough reason to bet on the race or whether it would be better to pass it by and find a race where there aren't such handicapping dilemmas.

When you find a race to handicap, start by evaluating speed. We'll use three calculations for speed. First of all, there's the speed in the very last race. Give the fastest horse a 3, the second fastest horse a 2 and the third fastest a

1. In the case of a tie, give each horse the lower number. So two horses tied for top speed would get a 2. Next, add the speed ratings for the last three races and then assign a number for each of the top three horses.

Finally, look at the top speed at the distance for each horse and once again assign a 3, 2, or 1 according to how well each horse did. Only the top three horses in each speed category should get a number, except in the case of when a horse is tied with another for third spot in which case they each get a 1. Now total the three speed categories and arrive at a final total for each horse. Obviously some horses won't have a speed number and they will be totally disregarded.

Next, divide the number of races each horse has run by the total amount of money each horse has earned and then write those amounts beside each horse. Starting with the highest average money earner, assign a 3 for the top money earner and a 2 for the next best and finally a 1 for the third best money earner. Handle ties the same way we handled them for speed ratings. Next, add the purse value of the last three races of each horse and put that total beside each runner.

Assign a 3 for the highest purse total for

the last three races and so on with the second and third highest totals. Add both class numbers together. You now have a class hierarchy from the best to the second best and so on. The same is true of speed. Now add speed and class together and you should arrive at a very good estimate of the class and speed in the race, probably the two most important factors.

2.
Horse Racing Secrets That Cost You Money

Many people look at the horse races as simple entertainment. They go to the races or OTB parlor and make some bets and try to get lucky. The races are entertaining and the colorful people you meet at the horse races are often worth the price of admission. Did you ever really think of what is going on at the track? When you place a bet, it's a pari-mutuel wager, meaning you're betting against the other players.

Would you sit down at a poker table without asking yourself who the other players were? If so, you must be a rank amateur because in any game, in order to have the best chance of winning, you should know your opponent better than he or she knows you. Obviously, you can't know all the people at the race track, but you can have an idea of where the money is coming from and who you're playing against.

Look around you at the races and ask yourself how many people are connected in some way with the horses and how many are directly involved in the races. The owners may not have inside information about every horse in the race, but many of them do have more information than you have about at least one horse in the race.

At almost any race track a lot of the money that's wagered on almost any race is inside money. Think of all the people who have access to information that isn't in the racing forms or programs. Did you go to the workouts for the last thirty days and watch the horses work in the morning? You can bet that some of the people you're betting against did.

Do you know which jockey is having personal problems and is therefore distracted and not likely to ride his or her best today? Once again, there are people who have that information. In fact, there are as many pieces of data and information that affect the outcome of the race that are not in the past performances or racing programs as there are bits of info that are in the program.

That means that you're at a distinct disadvantage unless you learn to watch the money and think about what it means and how it's spread around. The timing of bets is critical and so are the actual amounts in each pool, specifically how that money is disbursed. For instance, is there a higher percentage of money in the show pool on a certain horse than there is in the win pool?

What does that mean? Where did the money come from? The best way to handle these horse racing mysteries is to watch the races and the pools for at least a month and keep notes. Watch the betting action and then see what happens in the races. After a while you'll learn what it means and the mysteries will be solved. That means you will finally understand what's really happening and who is behind it.

3.
Using Campaigns to Make Good Bets On Horse Races

If you're looking for some good horse racing bets you may want to consider a few points before putting your money down. First and foremost of all, just what is a good bet? I know many people will tell you that any wager that wins is a good one, but actually, that's not really true. When it comes to making money on horse races, the pros are very selective about which wagers they make and when.

The most important part of being a successful horse player is good money management. That means getting the most value for your wagering dollar. It isn't easy even though the math is quite simple. If you learn to think of your bets in groups, sets, or campaigns, you'll be able to manage much better and may eke out a profit, though it's difficult to do for an extended length of time.

The reason you should think of your betting as a campaign and keep your campaigns limited to about twenty wagers is because it will allow you to quickly see any mistakes you're making and also help you to keep track of your money. If you don't have a way of monitoring your performance and making adjustments, how will you ever improve?

One thing you'll quickly see if you're looking at a set of wagers is which race types you're making the most money on and which ones you're losing on. While it may be expensive at first, I think it's best to start by playing many types of races such as maiden claiming races, maiden special weight races, allowance races, starter handicaps, and stakes races. Of course, it's also wise to make small bets until you can start to narrow it down.

Another possibility is to have a separate campaign for each track or race type. You may play twenty maiden claiming races and then start to narrow down your picks. Eventually you'll find that a good bet is one that you can make twenty times and show a profit on after all those races. If you keep your campaigns limited to certain kinds of races and keep accurate notes about the bets you make, you'll have a better chance of making a profit.

Just remember, however, that no matter how meticulous you may be, making a profit on horse races is very difficult and wagering on them is risky. Make every dollar count.

4.
How to Find a Good Horse Racing Bet

Are you trying to make a profit betting on horse races and your handicapping? If so, you probably know by now that most of the money is wagered on the favorite and the money is what the game is all about. Learn how to follow the money and beat the people who spend the most and you'll have a chance, though it's still risky and tough to make a go of it.

That means that the first step in finding a profitable wager is to look at the horse with most of the money on it and figure out if it's really worth all that confidence. Some people call the ones that don't deserve that support vulnerable favorites or false favorites. The favorite doesn't always have to have a flaw to be a poor betting choice.

What determines whether or not it's a good bet is whether its probability of winning is higher or lower than the actual payoff figure indicates. For instance, if you practice handicapping and watch enough races you'll develop the ability to know how often a runner with the favorite's attributes will win a race. For the sake of our example, let's say you think the horse that is the people's choice has a 50-50 chance of winning.

Let's also say it's at 2-1 at post time. That means out of ten races, based on a $1 bet, it would return $15 for every $10 wagered on it. In that case, it will be hard not to bet on the favorite rather than another horse. However, if it was at 3-5 odds it would become a poor wager and it would be time to find another horse that has a chance to win and will return good money.

The best place to start your search for such a horse is in the next two betting choices. Statistically they have the best chance of winning, after the chalk that is. Once again, just like you did with the top horse, you must determine what the chances, or odds, are of each of those horses winning and compare it to the actual odds.

Whether you're using a horse racing handicapping system, playing spot plays, or using any other method to pick your horses, the way to actually come out ahead is always the same. You have to know the chances of each horse winning and compare it to the actual odds on the tote board at post time. You must also allow some wiggle room on that because the odds may go even lower on the last click of the tote when you can no longer bet.

5.
Across the Board Horse Racing Betting Strategy and Best Bets

The across the board bet is one of the simplest wagers to make. If you're at a race track you simply tell the teller, or tote, that you want to bet a horse across the board. If you're using a machine or computer it may be marked as, "WPS," meaning win, place, and show.

If the runner manages to finish first, second, or third, you collect something. There are many things to be considered, however, before making the wager. First of all, just because you collect when the horse finishes in the money, it doesn't mean you'll make a profit. Many horses pay less than $6 to show and that's the cost of a base bet when you put $2 across the board on a horse.

Which horses should you bet across the board? Most of the time, you should only make that wager on a long shot that will pay at least $6 to show, but that betting strategy only works if the runner is not being backed heavily in the show pools. Sometimes, even though a horse is a long shot, the bettors will put quite a bit of money on it to place and show because they believe it has a chance to finish in the money.

There are enough people who bet long shots to place or show, hoping to catch a horse that is under bet and that will pay well in the second or third position, to make it necessary to check the pools if you're looking for the best bet. Unless you have access to information about those pools, however, this reasoning is often faulty because there will be a higher percentage of the show pool or place pool wagered on the horse than there is win money.

The best bet to place or show is a horse that is taking less money in the place or show pool than it's taking to win. Since those pools normally have less money than the win pool, this is best represented by a percentage. If you're looking for an easy bet that will have three chances to payoff, then the wps bet is a possibility, but if you're looking for a profitable bet, checking the percentages and then choosing a horse that is taking some action in the win pool, but that is taking a smaller percentage in the place or show pool is probably a better wager.

Just remember that there are no guarantees in life and any bet on a horse race involves risk.

6.
Basic Horse Racing Handicapping Steps to Find the Best Bet

There are no guarantees in horse racing so it becomes a matter of percentages and probability when you're trying to make a profit betting on horse races. It takes practice, patience, and discipline to finally reach the point where you can handicap a whole program and find enough good wagers to walk out of a race track or OTB parlor with a profit. If you're sitting at home and playing the races on your computer, the same is true.

To begin with, if you want to make money playing horses, you must realize that not every race has a good bet in it. You'll have to sit out some of the races. That's part of that discipline I mentioned earlier. Deciding if a race is playable is the first step in handicapping. You must be able to accurately gauge each horse's chances of winning by looking at the basic handicapping factors of speed, class, pace, recent form, and the trainer and jockey of each runner. If you can't quantify each of those attributes for a runner in the race, then you should probably pass the race. If there are two such runners, you should definitely pass the race.

Once you determine a race is playable, the next step is to look at the morning line and get an idea of which runner might be the favorite. Of course, with some experience you'll also be able to do this by looking at the basic factors. As you compare the speed in the last three races for each runner, you'll soon find that some horses are running faster in their recent races than others. Comparing them to the favorite, the trick is to determine which ones can beat the favorite.

If the horse that will take most of the betting money because it appears to be the fastest has a knock against it, then that horse may be a false favorite. The most likely knock is that the horse hasn't raced recently or that it has never won at the distance or on that surface. Races with a false favorite offer the best value.

Another important step is to determine the class of each horse. Class means the purse value of a race and how well the horse performed in that race. For instance, a horse that finished in the money in a $20,000 race would be considered competitive in a $16,000 race because it had finished well in a tougher race. Use the class and speed totals to make your own morning line for each horse based on how likely you think that runner may be to win and also how much it must pay to make it profitable.

The profit is based on how often the horse would win if the same race was run ten times. If it would win once in ten then the odds should be 10-1. If it would win twice in ten races then the odds should be 5-1. Use your own morning line to watch the tote board odds and find a horse that is at higher odds than your own morning line at post time.

7.
Horse Racing Tips for Cold Weather and Off Tracks

Horses appear to have short hair and some people therefore think that they are warm weather animals, but that isn't true at all. If allowed to free range in a field without a blanket on chilly days, horses quickly grow a longer coat of hair, and yes, it is hair, not fur. In fact, they love the cold. That being said, however, it's important to factor in the weather and track condition when you're handicapping a race.

As in all situations regarding horses, some are better at racing on an off track or in extreme cold. One thing that seems to be true of horses, as with all athletes, is that they must warm up before they race. Horses that are early speedsters seem to fare better on a warmer day than the closer type of horse.

Muscles cramp on the early speed horses and though they may get a good start in a race, as their muscles warm up and they get into their rhythm, the horses who come from off the pace often do well on a very cold day. Of course, the cold also affects the track condition. When it's very cold and the track is hard and fast, maybe even frozen in spots, that favors horses who like a hard dry surface.

It would seem that a hard track would favor speed and some tracks, like Aqueduct's inner track, for instance, do favor early speed in some situations. However, early speed may just be a horse with tactical speed that runs near the front, but not necessarily on the lead.

The best tip for handicapping races on a very cold winter day is to treat it as an off track and realize that some horses, those that handle the extreme cold the best, will have an advantage. Before playing any races on a day when the temperature is abnormally low, check the results from other days with similar weather conditions and see if there is a bias to a running style or post position.

You'll often find that the inside posts have a strong advantage on days when the mercury is very low. Another good angle is to look for horses that have won on days when the same conditions existed. There are horses that do not race during the summer and only race once the seasons change. At tracks like Aqueduct there are horses that start to race in November and once they are in condition win many races in December and January.

8.
Are there Any Good Horse Racing Systems

There are literally thousands of horse racing handicapping systems available for sale and many other people who sell horse racing picks and tips. Wending your way through the mine field of losers and winners isn't easy and can be expensive. I've been playing the horses and writing my own horse racing systems for years and here are some thoughts on the subject of winning and losing based on my own experience.

This is, of course, anecdotal, but may help you to find a good way to play the horses without losing your mind or your shirt. Here's the number one lesson or rule I've learned in years of owning and betting on horses...

Anything will work some of the time, but nothing works all the time.

That isn't double talk and though it's simple, it's one of those golden rules you should never forget. You may buy a horse racing system and start winning with it and think that you've finally found the key to the mint. Then you get the brilliant idea of putting your life's savings on the line or maybe mortgaging the house and wagering all that money. It seems like you can't lose because your system has been winning non-stop. Believe me, it can lose and will, if you give it enough time, because there's something else I've learned over the years...

Just when you think you can't lose, that you've found a winning system, you will. I'm not sure how it works, but somewhere in the universe there's a giant switch, like a light switch, and it controls that system. As you're dreaming about the fortune you're about to make and rushing to make that huge bet with money you really can't afford to lose, there's a hand reaching for that switch in order to shut it off. It still never ceases to amaze me how fast a winning streak can turn into a losing streak.

Now please don't get me wrong. I'm not saying you shouldn't try some horse racing systems or try to learn how to handicap horse races. What I'm telling you is that a good handicapping system will teach you some very useful methods and strategies, but will not necessarily guarantee you a profit without some skill on your part. You, as the handicapper, must decide when to wager and when not to wager and you must also determine which system to use on any particular day.

That takes time and patience and experience. My advice is to learn a few good systems and then follow them until you know when to play each one and when to lay off them. That's the whole key to making money with systems.

9.
How to Be Lucky At The Horse Races

There's no doubt about it, luck plays a big role in our daily lives whether we want to admit it, or not. If you go to the horse races and make a few bets you'll soon learn that luck is an important part of success. Preparation and hard work are important if you want to make a profit betting on horse races, but without luck, they're useless.

Here are a few horse racing tips related to luck based on my years of experience, both the good and bad. First of all, no one can control luck. Like lightning and athlete's foot, it just happens. So don't get too caught up in the game of trying to make luck happen, but do spend time trying to figure out when it will happen. It seems to come in cycles. I've often found that a really lucky day at the races is followed by a losing day.

So if you have a great day at the races, don't return the next day and start betting heavily right away. Luck is fickle and can turn on you in the blink of an eye. You can't control it, but you can welcome it into your life. Start by thinking about lucky people that you know and share something with them. Ask a lucky friend to spend a day at the horse races with you and listen and watch that friend to see how and why he or she bets.

You can also bet on lucky people and lucky horses. While many successful trainers and jockeys do work very hard at their careers, there's no denying it, the best all have more than their share of luck. So when you bet on the best you're more likely to share in that luck. I'm not talking about backing low priced favorites with the top jockey aboard, but you can rest assured that a good jockey on a top trainer's horse always has a chance no matter how bleak the outlook may appear on paper.

Racing luck is what happens on the track. A hole opens up on the rail and a smart jockey who waited patiently behind the leaders slides through to win with a long shot or there's an accident that takes out the top horses and leaves that horse that ran well off the pace to finish the race on top. The same people and horses who have racing luck are your partners when you bet on them.

Look at the running lines and see which horses and riders seem to have a gift for being in the right place and avoiding trouble in a race. Their luck will become your luck when you bet on them. Preparation is also important so learn what you can about handicapping and finding good bets using a simple system you can master in a reasonable amount of time.

10.
The First Step in Horse Racing Handicapping and Finding Winning Bets

Horse racing handicapping is broken down into steps based on the factors of evaluating a horse and then comparing each runner in a race to the competition. There are many ways to go about it, but one thing is certain, the better you become at making those comparisons the easier it will be to make a profit betting on horses.

Easier, but not easy, that is, because making a profit betting on horses is not easy. Not only do you have to make the comparisons I've just mentioned, but you also have to use that information, the disparity in ability and form between the runners, to find a good bet. Just because one horse seems to be in better condition and seemingly can run faster than the other horses, it doesn't mean that one is the one you should wager on.

If that doesn't seem to make sense, consider this, no horse is a guaranteed winner because of racing luck and the vagaries of fate. If horse A is the fastest and would easily win the same race six out of ten times if you ran it that many times, it doesn't mean that horse is a good bet. You have to consider the odds. Finding winning horses is fun, but identifying profitable bets is the key to making money on the horses.

Before you can do that, however, you also have to start the handicapping process. I recommend you do it in a systematic way which means you'll need some kind of system. If not, you're just groping around in the dark hoping to get lucky. The people who actually walk out of the OTB or race track with more money than they started with most of the time are the ones who have some skill at finding good bets. Luck will only take you so far in life.

Not every race should be played, in fact, after you've scanned the racing form, you will find that you shouldn't even waste your time handicapping some races. That's the first step. Identify the races that have too many unknown variables. Which races?

While maiden races offer opportunities for finding a good bet, because they're mostly based on raw speed, any maiden race with two or more first time starters is a race you should pass. You just can't evaluate those unknown runners properly. On the other hand, if each runner in a maiden race, particularly a maiden claiming event, has had at least two races, then handicap the speed and you'll often find a good bet.

While the outcome of any race is unknown until the race is declared official, there are some unknown bits of information that should tell you to pass a race. If the race is a claiming race and several horses are on their first or second race after the claim, be very wary. The form they showed in past races may change dramatically.

11.
Horse Racing Bets and Tips That Pay Off

There are thousands of tipping services and many ways to use their tips to bet on horse races. Every day, all over the world, people pay for tips and try to make a profit betting on the races. Most of them wind up losing money and yet, those services usually stay in business. Some offer more free tips if the ones you've paid for don't pay off. That doesn't seem to make sense, does it?

I'm not saying that all tipping services are bad or that any of them aren't worth a try, but I am saying that you should be very careful before paying for tips. Some of the best advice you can find for success at the race track can be found in free articles at horse racing sites and in the form as well as the public handicappers who often do offer some very good insights.

Putting it all together is the hard part and requires work and that's why many people never manage to get it all together and make money betting on horses. It's human nature to take the path of least resistance. So they continually look for that person or company who will give them winners. For most people, that's not going to happen.

If you want to really make money at the horse races you have to have excellent inside information and keen business sense to manage your money or you have to work very hard to learn good handicapping systems and then get the experience it takes to know when to use each one of them. That's the best tip you'll ever get on the horses and it's free.

There are several types of systems and the easiest ones are those that teach you how to scan a program for spot plays. Spot plays often pay off because they're horses that are in a particular situation that has historically proven to be profitable. That doesn't mean they're a dead cert. or that things won't change, but it's a possibility. You have to pay attention to trends at the track and decide if the spot plays will hold up.

The best advice is to learn some systems and master money management. Then follow one or two race tracks and get to know the peculiarities of that track and watch for biases and trends. It's work. For most people, making money involves work, even though some love the work and the challenge, it's still work. If you just want to gamble and try to be lucky, there's nothing wrong with that as long as it does not get to be an obsession or becomes destructive in your life. If you want to be a successful horse player and really make money at it, you're going to have to work at it.

Now, that's just my opinion, but I've been at the business many decades. Whatever you do, remember this, there are no sure things and never gamble with money you can't afford to lose.

12.
Quick Handicapping Angles and A Simple and Easy Horse Racing System

There's no substitute for real in-depth handicapping if you want to make money betting on horse races, but if you don't have a lot of time and you want to estimate each horse's chance of winning, here's an angle that will help you to evaluate the runners. It's a quick and easy horse racing system.

Go through the program and circle the horse in each race with the fastest speed rating in its last race. Then put a 2 beside the horse with the second fastest rating and a 3 beside the horse with the third fastest rating in each race. Believe it or not, you've just narrowed your search down to about 70% of the winners that easily. In most horse races the winner is one of the top three horses according to their speed in their last race.

Next, look at the weight each horse is carrying today compared to what it carried last time out. Most winners add no more than two pounds. Look at your top three horses and put a line through any horse that is adding more than 2 pounds. I know it doesn't seem like a few pounds matters, but it does and statistics prove that fact.

You'll probably eliminate a few runners on the program just by getting rid of horses that are adding too much weight. The next way to eliminate horses that are bucking the trend is to look for horses that are coming back from a long layoff. Once again, statistically, they just don't win very often. Looking at your top contenders, the horses you circled or put a 2 or 3 beside, scratch out any who haven't raced in 45 days.

Now the next part is tricky. I usually eliminate horses that have a jockey with less than a 10% win average unless that rider has won on the horse recently. It's really a matter of judgment and you may or may not eliminate a horse depending upon your estimation of the rider's chances with that horse.

By this time you may have a race or two with no contenders and perhaps one or two with just one or two contenders. These are horses that it's reasonable to consider for a win bet. The whole process doesn't take very long and can be a lot of fun. If you can get a decent price on any of them you may come out ahead of the game.

It's a quick and easy system for handicapping a horse race and while it may not make you rich, it can make a day at the track a lot more fun without a lot of effort.

13.
How Important Is Class As A Horse Racing Handicapping Factor

Class is perhaps the most misunderstood and therefore most difficult handicapping factor to quantify and use successfully. That means that many people either misuse the information that's available or ignore it because they don't know how to use it to their advantage. Therefore, a select few who master class handicapping have an advantage over many of their peers. That's known as an edge in gambling.

Every gambler, whether a he or she is a horse player or a poker player, wants to have the edge. Spending some time and working at understanding what class is, how to spot it, and to make comparisons using it, is very important. Here are some thoughts on class.

First of all, just how important is it? In about 90% of races run in North America the winner is running at the same class as its last race or a lower class. In other words only about 10% of races are won by a horse moving up in class. At first, that sounds like a startling figure and it seems that all you have to do is eliminate the horses moving up in class and you've mastered handicapping, but statistics don't work that way.

You also have to ask yourself how many horses in a given race are actually moving up in class? If only ten percent of the horses that are racing are moving up in class then only about 10% of the races should be won by horses moving up. As it turns out, only about 20%-25% of horses are moving up in class on any given program and sometimes even less, depending on the track and the length of the meet.

But class is still a significant factor since only about a half or a third of those horses moving up can win. In order to accurately gauge the ability and quality of a runner you have to see how well it fared against horses at any level. For instance, if a horse finished 15 lengths behind the leader in a $20,000 claiming race and showed no decent position at any of the calls of the race, you wouldn't consider it a contender at a slightly lower level, say $15,000. However, if it managed to run within 4 lengths of the winner in that

$20,000 race a slight drop in class might make it competitive.

If you want to find the true class of any runner, always search its past races until you find a race where it successfully contested the pace for at least two calls or finished within a few lengths of the eventual winner. You must also consider the time factor when doing so and if that race was over 90 days ago, look to see how much the horse has run since then and whether its form is declining by noting any upward or downward trend in speed figures.

14.
Horse Racing Winners System Based on Class and Speed

While speed often does win races, it isn't foolproof and just basing your horse racing handicapping decisions on speed alone will often fail. The reason for that is that class horses often don't show they're true speed because they're dropping out of races where they were over matched into races they can dominate.

The process of accurately estimating a horse's true ability, its projected speed in the upcoming race, is a process of finding the right balance of speed and pace adjusted for the quality of the competition. The problem with this is that there are no hard and fast rules or an accurate scale that can be used. It becomes a matter of personal experience.

However, while the rating of that class horse that is dropping into today's race is problematic, one thing is almost always true. If you put a class horse that has demonstrated speed at a higher class into a race, it's almost always a top contender. On the other hand, it's hard to find such runners at reasonable odds.

My system for evaluating horses in races is based on many factors. Sometimes I just find a spot play that meets certain conditions which I call filters. If a horse can make it through the filters I consider it a contender. The filters are based on recent form, how many days ago it raced, class, (it can't be moving up), and speed, (it must be in the top three).

I also like to see that the jockey has won with the horse before or that he or she has at least an 11% win average. Statistically, horses in the top three in the morning line have about a 70% chance of winning. That means one of the three will win the race about seven out of ten times. So it doesn't hurt to see that the horse is in the top three. They usually are if they can make it through those filters.

If, for some reason, the horse is at longer odds, that doesn't mean I dismiss it or it can't win. Quite to the contrary, it means that there is some cloud over the horse that makes the odds maker doubt its chances or there are three other horses in the race that appear better. This is the time for experience to kick in and the good handicapper must check out the competition to see if the runner is really over matched or the odds maker has made a mistake.

Sometimes, when a horse makes it through the filters and yet is at long enough odds, it becomes a very good bet.

15.
Horse Racing System Basics to Find Winners and Best Bets

While a good horse racing system for handicapping the races does require some work and effort in order to succeed, there are some basics that are very simple that every horse player should know before betting. The reasons to use a handicapping system are obvious since anything that we do in life requires some thought to get the steps in the right order. Without a little planning almost anything is more difficult and more likely to fail.

The basics of handicapping and betting are based on statistics and money management. The statistics relate to the sport itself while the money management guidelines may be applied to almost any investment. While it may be fun to pick winners and make wagers, it's important that you realize that without taking care to manage your money well, you may still lose financially even when you pick the best of bets.

Therefore, learn how to pick winners but also learn how to pick bets. Good bets are the ones that have a positive ROI or return on investment. Profitable bets are found by first estimating the horse's chances of winning using the statistics based on handicapping factors such as speed, class, form, and the connections (jockey and trainer). After you've determined the horse's chances, the next step is to turn that into odds. Establish your own morning line based on what you think the horse's real chance of winning may be.

For instance, after you compare the basic handicapping factors if you decide that the runner has a fifty-fifty chance of winning, then fair odds would be 1-1. Now look at the odds on the tote board just before post time and see if they're higher or lower than 1-1. If the horse is at odds of say, 9-5, then you can expect to make money. If you stick to horses that are going to post at odds that are higher than your morning line you should make money in the long run.

How do you make the comparisons between handicapping factors and turn that into odds? That takes practice with a good system that evaluates runners or locates a horse that is in a favorable position to win, meaning that the factors indicate it's superior to the other runners. There are no guarantees that it will win and betting on horse races is always risky, but a good system and good money management are keys to success in any investing opportunity. Start by mastering a few good horse racing systems.

16.
Horse Racing Betting Strategy for Wheeling Horses

If you're serious about making money betting on horses you will not only have to learn to handicap so you can evaluate the runners and compare them to each other, but you'll also have to learn how to bet to get the most profit for the risks that you take. In other words, you'll have to learn how to handicap and how to bet.

Wagering on races is fun, but can also be risky. It may be profitable and a lot of what you get out of it depends on the kind of person that you are. The risks that you take will be directly related to your comfort level and need for that adrenaline rush from plunking down cold hard cash and watching a race. One popular way to wager on races is the wheel bet, or wheeling.

Wheeling means that you place a horse on top in an exotic bet, such as the exacta or trifecta and then if that horse wins, you win, though what you win depends not only on the odds of your wheel horse, but also on the odds of the horses that complete the exotic bet. That's really throwing caution to the wind and taking a gamble because, while you may know the odds on your top horse, you'll have no idea which horses may complete the bet and therefore, you won't have a clue as to what the wager may return.

Wheeling is a win bet on steroids and without filters. It may seem easy at first because you don't have to go to the trouble of figuring out which horses to play with your horse as you do when you play a key bet and key the horse over a select group of horses, but you pay for that ease with a lot of combinations that don't and can't come in.

For instance, in a trifecta bet with your horse wheeled on top in an 8 horse race, there are 42 possible combinations that may come in, but when the race is finally official, only one of them will pay off. That means that you've spent an extra $41.00 (if you play a dollar trifecta wheel), for nothing. On the other hand, if you can narrow it down to four possible horses that may complete the trifecta the wager only costs $12.

The problem, of course, is that the very

horses you eliminate because they appear to have no chance, will pay the most if they do manage to get into your trifecta. Leaving out long shots means you'll miss the big payouts and only hit the smaller trifectas. Admittedly, you'll cash more tickets, but will you make a profit?

Depending upon your ability to take risks and sit through some losing streaks, I recommend a compromise. Key your top horse over 4 other horses for that $12 bet, but instead of using just the top four horses, play two horses that figure to run well and see if you can find two others that have a reason, no matter how slight it may appear, to run in the money. It's a compromise between gambling and handicapping.

17.
Find the Best Bet in Horse Racing That Pays the Most for the Smallest Bet

Learning how to bet on horse races and to get the best bet for maximum profit is not easy, but can be done with patience and practice. One of the biggest obstacles to making money at the horse races is that there are so many different kinds of wagers and ways to play the ponies. For the beginner or even for seasoned players, it's difficult to choose the best way to proceed.

Here are some thoughts on how you can use a little bit of money to get the most. First of all, don't be greedy. Be realistic. If you don't have a lot to risk, then you probably won't get rich over night. Another thing to consider is that betting on horse races is always risky. There are no sure things in life, especially when gambling is part of the recipe. Therefore, only risk what you can afford to lose.

There's an old maxim at the track. It goes

something like this, "Scared money never wins." What does that mean? It means that when you're afraid of losing you play the races differently than when you're willing to really take a chance. So don't get out of your comfort zone.

Should you bet exotic bets like the pick threes and fours and trifectas or should you stick with straight bets like win, place, and show? You can bet dime supers that only cost ten cents per combination. At first these bets such as dime supers, fifty cent trifectas, and others that seem to cost just nickels and dimes seem to offer the best chances for big payoffs for small wagers. Before you decide to try them, however, remember this, in a ten horse race a $1 win bet on any horse has a one out of ten chance of winning (handicapping considerations aside) and costs just one dollar.

In an eight horse race keying the same horse on top and wheeling it in the $1 trifecta means the same bet will cost you $42. That horse still has the same chance of winning, but in order for the wager to be more profitable than a straight win wager, the dollar trifecta payoff has to equal 42 times the win payoff. In my experience, that usually doesn't happen.

Therefore, I still recommend betting on a horse to win. Which horse should you wager on? Unless you have a good handicapping system or handicapping knowledge the best horses to wager on are the first three in the odds on the board at two minutes to post. That is, they have the best chance of winning, you'll often find the winner in their ranks. To narrow it down even more, check the morning line and then compare it to actual odds on the board.

You can play it either of two ways. You can bet on the one that is at the highest odds compared to the morning line, or the one that is bet down lower than its morning line odds. The ones bet down below their morning line odds have the greater chance of winning, but they'll pay less, while those above the morning line may actually be a good bargain and show a profit for the day.

18.
Easy Horse Racing Handicapping Methods Using Speed

Speed is the key to horse racing handicapping, but how do you use it to find the best bets? Finding the bets that really pay off, the ones you can make a profit on, isn't easy at the races. Favorites often win, but seldom do they pay enough so that you can show a profit at the end of the day if you stick with the public's choice in each race.

One of the best horse racing tips I can give you is that at the horse races, you have to be flexible. You must use a different method on different types of races and in particular situations. Learning how to handicap horse races means learning when to use each speed handicapping method.

One approach is to look for horses that are consistent. No other single indicator points out the consistent runner than an average speed rating. If you add the rating for the last three races for each runner in the race, then take the top three, you'll probably have the winner within that group at least 70% of the time. Of course, the tricky part is then to figure out which one to bet on. That takes time and experience but there are worse ways to narrow down the field to find the true contenders.

While the average method works well in many races, there are times when you must abandon that method in favor of another way to pick winners. Once you've averaged their ratings it's a good idea to go back and look at the progression of the ratings for each runner. Sometimes you'll notice that they're going up and other times they may be going down.

For instance, if the horse's last three ratings were 70, 75, 80 with the 80 being the most recent, you'd figure that the horse was improving. It means that the runner may actually do better today than that 80 rating and certainly better than the average of 75 which it has for its last three races.

If you find a horse that is improving in such a manner, it may be a good bet. While those handicappers who pay attention to form may also spot that pattern of improvement, many of the horse players in the crowd may not.

The same is true of horses that have a pattern that shows a decline in form. If a horse that is in your top three average speed horses is going out of form, then that's one you can probably eliminate from your considerations.

Section 4:

1.
The Key to Horse Racing Betting Strategy For Profits

While learning how to handicap and evaluate the horses is important for success at the races, knowing a good bet when you see one is the real key and here's why...

There are many races all over the world every day, but many of them offer few if any real opportunities for making money for the handicapper. I know what you're thinking, there has to be a good bet in each race. There's usually only one winner, except in the case of a dead heat. The horse that wins is always a good bet as soon as the results are official.

Real successful horse players do not think like that and that's why they make money. They look at sets of bets or runs. For instance, a horse player may say, "I'm going to make twenty win bets in a set and a series of four sets to test my new strategy."

Those bets are based on finding value as expressed by probability and payoff. If a horse will win one race out of ten, that's the probability. If the horse is at 12-1 on the tote board at 0 minutes to post, that's the projected payoff. The problem of course, is that in arbitrage betting the odds may change significantly after the bell and the good bet may become a stinker.

Why is that a good bet? It's good because if you played a set of twenty such bets you'd have two winners that would pay $26 each for a total of $52. On the other hand, the actual set of bets would cost $40 based on $2 bets. That's a profit of $12 or an ROI (return on investment) of 30%. Then, you may ask, why can't the same handicapping strategy and investment strategy be used in any race?

Horse players play angles that they know have an expected strike rate. A strike rate is the number of times the horse with a certain angle or factors will win in a given set of races. The above example was one race out of ten. That would be quite a longshot, but longshot or favorite, the key is that the crowd, the other bettors have underestimated the runner's chances or probability. When the other bettors make a mistake calculating probability, the smart horse player makes money.

If you want to make a profit at the horse races, you must learn to estimate the probability of a runner winning based on its attributes. That's good handicapping. But be warned that making money betting on horse races is very difficult and risky.

2.
Who Wins Money at the Horse Races and How Do They Do It

If you've ever been to the horse races you've probably noticed that a lot of money changes hands in the course of a day. If you've wagered on a race and lost, you probably wondered who won your money. First of all, of course, the race track takes money out of each pool to pay itself and also any taxes that go to the state or municipality. It's called the "vig."

There's also something called breakage which is a fancy word for rounding off amounts so you're not getting paid in pennies. Guess who gets to keep the pennies?

Finally, the rest of the money is distributed to the bettors who won. If you take the time to meet some of the people at the races you'll find that a lot of them are connected in some way with the races. There are also people on the backstretch that you don't meet unless you have business back there. Those people may be grooms, hot walkers, trainers, vets, exercise riders, etc.

I don't know what the percentages are, but I can tell you that a lot of the people who bet on races also have an interest in them as well as inside information. Whoa, you say, they have information I don't have? That's right. While they don't know everything about every horse in a race or at the track, you can bet (if you dare) that they know some juicy things about the runners and jockeys and trainers that help them to have an edge.

Makes betting against them seem a little daunting, doesn't it?

Winning money consistently by betting on horse races is extremely difficult. Anyone who tries will tell you that. My own experiences haven't always been good, but I have learned from them. I've also been an owner and a groom. With the inside information I had from my time spent on the backstretch and the hard work I put in as a handicapper I could sometimes eke out a profit.

Being able to go to the backstretch and mingle with the horse people is one good way to learn things about the runners and the people who get them ready for the races. With all that information, however, a horse race is still unpredictable. While the insiders may know that a particular horse should win, it doesn't mean that he will. The same is true of lameness. Injuries usually slow horses down, but sometimes they win in spite of injuries or pain.

My advice to you, if you want to be one of the people who win at the horse races, is to find a way to become connected to the horses and people involved in the business. Like they say, if you can't beat them, join them.

3.
A Good Horse Handicapping Method Based on Impact Values

One of the problems that people encounter when they handicap a horse race is figuring out which factors to use and how important each one of those factors is. For instance, you may determine each horse's average speed and class, but which one is more important? The same may be said of running styles and post positions. Some providers of horse racing programs supply impact values to their customers.

Using their vast databases the data companies can look at thousands of races and measure the impact or effect that each factor contributed to the final result. An example would be a set of one thousand races at six furlongs for three year old fillies. The computer would determine the class and speed as well as running style for each runner in all those races. Then, looking at just the winners, patterns would start to emerge. For instance, how often does a horse with an early speed running style (E) win such races?

The complicated mathematical equations are used to arrive at an expected result based on the number of runners in the race. In a ten horse race each runner has a 10% chance of winning, if each runner has exactly the same skill and ability. Obviously, such races are rare or even non-existent. That's where the factors come into play. If horses with an E win 30% of the time the impact of the E is clearly seen.

The problem, of course, is that the number crunchers also have to look at the other factors that each of the E horses, whether winners or losers, had going for them. If some of the E's were in post positions that were more favorable, and therefore had a positive impact value, then that positive impact must be deducted from that 30%. Past speed and class would also have to be factored into the equation.

These types of calculations obviously require complex algorithms and are usually far beyond the average handicapper. That's why the programs with impact values are very helpful. Before you give up and concede that the computer is a better handicapper than you are, however, remember this, you can look at the horses and use your own experiences as a horse player to tweak that program and the impact values. While the final result of their calculations is often expressed as one number that is used to compare the runners to each other, you can take those comparisons and compare them to your own knowledge and intuition.

4.
What Successful Horse Racing Handicappers Look For in a Race

Millions of people handicap horse races every day, but how many of them really succeed at making a profit at the races? The answer is that very few people can make money betting on horse races, in my opinion. That opinion is based on decades of playing the races and studying the crowd. If so many people try but fail, what is it that the few who succeed possess that the others fail to see?

Many people are good handicappers, meaning that they can compare the horses and develop a hierarchy of ability that leads to an expectation of results or probability. While that is handy and can be used to develop a betting line, there are many races that are too close to call or where the difference between the horses is too slight. Wise and profitable handicappers back off at that point and look for an easier race that has what every gambler on the planet needs to succeed.

I'm writing about an **edge**. What kind of edge do I mean? There are two ways to describe it and two situations that must present themselves in order to make a wager on the race. The first edge is that advantage that a horse may have over the competition. One such example is a runner that has run and won at today's distance while the rest of the horses don't have that valuable experience. Finding one of these "been there done that," type horses in a race with an unproven field, means that runner has a decided edge in experience and therefore may win.

That fact alone, however, is not enough to make a professional horse player bet on that horse. This is where the second edge comes into the equation. The horse player will watch the horse's odds during the betting and will try to determine how the crowd, or betting public, is handling that situation. Are they betting the horse heavily? Is it being ignored because another runner has superior speed figures or some other compelling factor going for it?

If, in the handicapper's opinion, the odds are right for a horse with that edge, then he will probably bet on that runner. The proposition has two key facets. One, the horse has a reason to win. Two, the price offered on the horse indicates a positive betting situation. The fundamentals that all successful gambling wagers and situations are based on are the edges. You find the value on the edges and not in situations that are too close to call or where the money is spread too thin over many runners.

5.
Horse Racing Handicapping Factors Post Position and Running Style

While track models indicate advantageous running styles in some races, the way a horse runs and how it accelerates through a race may or may not benefit that runner depending upon another very important factor -- the post position.

Obviously, the runner on the inside, closest to the rail, the one path, has the advantage of having to cover less ground than any other runner. That is true as long as its path isn't blocked. But what if the inside horse is a closer with no early speed and early speedster horses race to the lead and move over in front of that horse? Even though the track model may indicate that closers, horses coming from off the pace, have the advantage, if it is in traffic, horses in front as well as to its outside, getting free to mount a run in the stretch may be difficult.

On the other hand, if the closer type horse is in an outside post position and will take an outside path, though it may have to cover more ground, it may still have a better trip and be more likely to succeed. Early speed, even in races where early speed doesn't have an advantage, may still enable a runner to win if the race shapes up the right way.

Of particular note are races with short runs to the first turn, especially routes. Some route races start close to the first turn. The run to that turn favors early speed on the inside. If a horse has good early foot, but is in an outside post position, it may expend too much energy in the run to the first turn in order to gun to the lead and cross to the rail.

A closer that gradually works its way into an easy path and then begins picking horses off will often do well in an outside post. It's up to the rider to figure out whether the horse should be urged to the lead early. That is often easier said than done, however and a headstrong horse, fighting the rider and struggling for the early lead from the outside, will often tire badly in the stretch and finish poorly.

As you handicap the race look for horses that may try for the lead but who will get caught out wide on the first turn because there is too much early speed inside of them. The race may be determined by a photo finish that is won or loss by a neck, head, or nose. Losing valuable ground and many feet or yards on the first turn may often be the difference between winning and losing.

6.
Jockey Switches and Handicapping Horse Races

Jockeys know the horses they ride better than just about anyone. They're the experts so when one of them has the choice of several horses in the race, the jock usually picks the best one. Of course, life and racing being what they are, they aren't always right and sometimes circumstances beyond the rider's control will result in a horse that was passed over winning the race.

The 2013 Kentucky Derby was an example of just such a choice that didn't work out well and the jockey in question is one of the best, John Velazquez. Johnny V., as he is called by his many fans, had ridden both Orb and Verrazano in previous races. I'm not sure that he made the decision, it may possibly have been made by one of the trainers or owners, but it was probably made by Johnny V. Verrazano was unbeaten and except for not having raced as a two year old, he certainly looked like a contender for favoritism.

On the other hand, Orb had won some big horses against the best of the three year old crop and was certainly no slouch. Orb won the race. It may be argued that Johnny V. didn't know that the track would be off when the race was finally won. He had to make his choice long before the weather forecast and also he may have adhered to the old rule, "Stick with a winner."

Whatever the case may be, though that is an example of a jockey making the wrong choice, it is not to be considered an indication of how you should make your decisions as a handicapper when you're handicapping a horse race that includes jockey switches. In the long run they're right more often than they're wrong. paying attention to which horses the rider's prefer will help you in your decision making process when picking winners.

It may not be a standalone method for handicapping, but it is one of the tools you can use to come to an opinion about how a horse stacks up against the others in the race.

This is particularly true if there are several horses in a race and you are having a problem rating each one against the other. Knowing which one a good jockey thinks is the better of the two can really help to narrow down your choice. Using this angle along with the other handicapping factors to evaluate the runners and then assign what you consider to be fair odds on them can lead to race track profits, as long as you also have a little luck.

7.
Handicapping Triple Crown Races For Three Year Olds In N. America

There are several series of races around the world known as the Triple Crown, but for the purposes of this article, we're talking only about the three races held in the United States every year for three year old thoroughbreds. They are the Kentucky Derby, Preakness Stakes, and The Belmont. Each race has its own characteristics because each one is held at a different race track over a different distance and at a different time in each runner's development.

Horses that race in the first race of the series, the Kentucky Derby, can only get there by making enough money in graded stakes races to qualify for the race. The field is usually large, but many hundreds of three year old hopefuls who were eligible for the Derby have already been weeded out by the earnings requirements, injuries, or other factors.

About twenty thoroughbreds (usually but not exclusively male) will go to post on the first Saturday in May at historic Churchill Downs in Kentucky and minutes after the starting gate opens, a new Kentucky Derby winner is crowned and the pulses of millions of horse racing fans quicken as they wonder if this newest racing star will be the next one to win all three races in the series and become the next Triple Crown Champion. There haven't been many in the hundred and thirty plus years the race has been run and the twenty first century has yet to see one.

So how do you, the handicapper choose the next winner of the Derby? Wait. Wait until the prep races have been run and the stage is set. Don't be duped into thinking that a fantastic performance in one of those stakes races leading up to the Derby means a three year old is unbeatable. That's often the case and it leads to many favorites in the Derby losing and disappointing millions of people.

The truth of the matter is that you want to spot the horse with the right breeding that is going to peak on the first Saturday in May, not the horse that ran its best race in March of April.

If any series of races ever tested a handicapper's ability to project into the future, to prognosticate based on the past, it's the Triple Crown races. First and foremost, the horse has to be bred to go the distance. Secondly, it must have a champion's blood (which they usually do) and finally, it must have a lot of racing luck. For that look to the rider and trainer and how lucky they have been in the past.

Look for a horse that seems to be improving with each race that also seems to have not hit his or her best race late.

8.
Using Track Eccentricities to Handicap Horse Races

A good handicapper handicaps the track as well as the horses. Just as no two people on earth are exactly alike, no two places on earth are exactly alike. This is true of race tracks and can be used to your advantage if you're wise enough to pay attention. The big tracks are known to have their quirks. For instance, some handicappers believe that the track at Del Mar is influenced by the nearby ocean and tides that they say run under the surface of the oval.

The factors that contribute to a race track's nature are shape of the track, including the angle of the turns and the length of the home stretch. The composition of the racing surfaces also add to the chances of something being unique. The grass tracks may be dryer or harder at one venue than they are at another.

Some players won't make a bet until they've watched a few races to determine if front runners or closers are winning. If there is a bias, they want to be able to spot it. There have been days in my own horse playing career when I failed to note a bias that played all day and I paid for it with my losses. In order to be competitive a horse player must pay attention and use every edge.

In my opinion, the best tracks to put this strategy to good use are the smaller secondary tracks. While all tracks have them, the smaller tracks seem to be quirkier and the crowds seem to miss it more often. Weather is a particularly helpful phenomenon to the horse player who is smart enough to use it and who is patient enough to use it. Knowing that two inches of rail destroys the running path along the rail and benefits outside runners can make you a lot of money, but only under those special conditions that only come along once in a while.

The best way to use this method of handicapping is to choose several of your favorite tracks and familiarize yourself with their actual dimensions. If you know that a horse that has a good kick in the homestretch is moving to a track with a longer stretch run, then you know that runner may do better today and will benefit from the added distance. You'll only know that, however, if you know the stats of the tracks.

Another factor is the weather and how it affects horses from different post positions and with different running styles. In order to profit from those special situations you'll need to keep notes and know how your track plays in all kinds of weather. You also still have to pay attention to the other handicapping factors when you evaluate the runners.

9.
Handicapping In The Spring When Tracks Are "Muddy" Or "Off"

April showers may bring May flowers, but to horse racing handicappers they also bring headaches and problems in the form of off tracks that are listed as muddy, sloppy, or that most deceptive of all terms, good. A good track does not mean that the track is dry and fast and the footing is good. It simply means that it isn't wet enough to be listed as muddy or sloppy, but it also isn't fast.

There are different ways to handle the off track problem. You can simply not bet on any races at the track on that day. With all the simulcasting now available you can usually find a track somewhere that is listed as fast if you really feel you can't get through the day without handicapping and betting on a horse race. For some of us, however, a day without horse racing is a day without sunshine.

The next approach is to play the horses that you feel are "mudders." *Mudders* are horses who have shown some talent running on a muddy or sloppy track. Good long shot bets can sometimes be found among the horses who have been struggling to win on a fast track but who are fond of wet surfaces. The reasons are varied but one possible reason is that the horse is lame and the softer track is easier on sore legs.

Another suggestion is simply that the horse, due to its conformation and shape of its hooves, is well suited to get traction and run well in mud. There are theories about small hooves and large hooves and shape of the hooves and even the way a horse places its hoof on the track as it races. Whatever the case may be, there's no denying that some horses just run better when the going is wet.

When looking for runners who will be able to handle the surface, however, remember this, just because the track is off you can't throw recent form and conditioning out the window. The fit, sharp, and ready horse still has the advantage, even on an off track. If a horse hasn't ever run on a wet track before you may get clues as to how it will handle the track surface from its breeding.

Some past performances and many breeding guides give information about how the sire and dam sire fared on wet tracks. The final clue is the fact that the trainer has decided not to scratch the horse. If the conditioner of the horse thinks it should race on an off track, it may mean that he or she has confidence that the horse will handle the off going well, or at least it's worth the risk to try it and find out how it likes an off track.

10.
Horse Racing Handicapping Angles and Tips for Class and Speed

Learning how to handicap horse races can be very fulfilling, but it's also very difficult to become skilled enough to actually make money as a horse player. The key to becoming a better horse player than the average punter is to acquire knowledge that the crowd doesn't use and then to understand how to use that knowledge creatively to find good bets.

One way you can become a better handicapper is by familiarizing yourself with the differences in the class levels at the race tracks you like to play. While generally speaking the horses running in $10,000 claiming races will be about the same as those at another race track running at the same level, there are some differences.

At each race track there is a hierarchy of class and speed and sometimes there are very big differences between each level. For instance, the jump up from the $5,000 claiming level to the $6,250 level may be much more difficult than the next move to the $8,000 level. Truly understanding the differences in talent and ability between each class at your favorite track will help you to evaluate the runners as they move up and down the class ladder.

An example would be a horse dropping from the $15,000 level to the $10,000 level after a mediocre performance and finishing 5 lengths back in his last race. If you know that there is a very big difference in the caliber of horses running in $15,000 claiming races you may know that the horse that is dropping will be an easy winner if he equals his last speed rating.

However, if you realize there isn't much difference in the two claiming levels as far as talent goes, you may assume he will not have an easy win and you may look for value in another bet. The average bettor at the track may see that class drop and think the runner will be an easy winner. If they bet that one down it means another horse may go to post at high enough odds to make it a good bet.

Sometimes the differences in talent and ability are so great that a double drop in class at one level is equal to a single drop at another level. The wise handicapper can use this information to have an edge over the competition. The information you have that will actually help you to make money betting on horses will usually be the information you have to do some digging for and that the rest of the crowd can't find. Other than inside information from a trainer or owner, that's the only way to win.

11.
Horse Racing Handicapping Using The Best Speed At the Distance

One of the many statistics that handicappers use to evaluate the runners in a race is, "the best speed at the distance statistic," also known as BSD. The BSD is the fastest speed figure that the horse earned at the same distance as the race it is about to run in and naturally, if the horse has never run at the distance, there is no information for the handicapper.

Knowing that a horse ran 6 furlongs at the fastest time can be very helpful when you're comparing the runners, but you do have to use some common sense when using that stat. First and most importantly, you should check to make sure the figure was earned on a fast, dry track. It's also important to know what surface the horse ran on. For instance, if the figure was earned on an All Weather track, it doesn't apply to turf or dirt. It does make a difference.

The age of the runner and how recently that figure was earned also matters. For instance, if the horse last raced at 6 furlongs when it was just two years old and now it is four, it will probably be able to run much faster. On the other hand, if the horse earned its BSD when it was three or four years old and is now much older, it may well be past its prime. The rigors of racing may have also taken their toll and the runner may not be able to race to that figure it earned earlier in its career.

Like all handicapping factors, the best speed at the distance should be used as one factor and holistically as well. You must use the other factors to adjust it up or down and pay attention to the nuances of the game. While some people like to see that the figure was earned recently, if it was earned too recently the horse may not race well.

Sometimes when horses put forth a great effort and score a high speed figure they "bounce," as it's called and run a sub-par race. The only way you'll be able to use the BSD as a way to pick good bets is with practice and experience. Just be sure to keep good notes so that you will be able to benefit from your experiences picking winners and handicapping races.

Remember that horses are living and breathing animals and not machines, so no two horses are exactly alike. Just because one set a fast time in the past it doesn't mean you are guaranteed a winner. However, if you use all the information available to you and proceed deliberately and cautiously, you may be one of the few who can make a profit betting on horse races.

12.
Using Trainer Moves Effectively to Pick Horse Racing Winners   Profitably

Picking a winning horse, but losing money in the long run is not a very efficient way to be a horse player. Your bankroll eventually runs out and you become a grumpy old man or woman who walks around the race track muttering to yourself. You may be wondering how you can lose money if you pick winners. It isn't hard to do. Here's how.

If you cash a ticket on half your bets but they pay less than even money, you'll lose money in the long run. If you win a third of the time that you bet but only average $5 winners, you'll lose money in the long run. Get the picture? The key to making money betting on horses is to be good enough to pick winners that pay enough to cover all your bets and to also make you a profit.

It isn't easy and that's why there are so many grumpy old men and women stumbling around the race tracks muttering to themselves.

That brings us to winning plays that pay enough to make a profit. If you follow trainers and their moves, the things they do to get a horse to win a race, you probably know that as soon as a good stat is known the past performances carry that information and each time the trainer tries that move so many people bet on the horse they drive the odds down to the point where it is a lousy bet. How then can you profit from trainer moves?

Each time a trainer tries one of his or her classic moves, such as dropping a horse in class, adding blinkers, changing distances, etc., you should note that horse's name and whether it wins or loses. If it wins it will probably win at very low odds. If it loses a lot of people will become disappointed, probably question the trainer's parentage, and become grumpier than they were before they bet on that horse.

The next time the horse runs most of the people will either forget about the horse or be so burned up because they lost money on it that they will not bet on it. The odds will go up, but remember this, that trainer thought the horse was good enough to win that last race. A good trainer is a good judge of a horse's condition. If the horse races back in thirty days, even if it doesn't appear as though the trainer is trying anything special, it may be a very good bet.

13.
How to Pick Winning Horses by Spotting Big Changes and Trainer Moves

If you want to find a way to pick winning horses that pay well you need to learn what to look for, how to handicap in a way to that points out horses that will surprise most of the crowd. Long shots are not hard to find, but long shots that have a chance of winning are few and far between. Here are some tips that may help you to find winning bets.

First of all, let's talk about what you should not do at the horse races or any where else in life. Do not keep repeating the same mistakes and expect different results. If you keep going to the horse races and betting the same old way and expect to somehow start winning, you're just kidding yourself. Start right now by telling yourself that something has to change because like they say, "The definition of insanity is doing the same thing over and over and expecting different results."

Not only do you have to change, but you also have to be able to figure out when a horse is going to change its performance. Of course, that means some human intervention from the trainer. Changes are the key to cashing winning tickets. First of all, however, you need to know when what appears to be a little change could make a big difference and when a little change will have little effect.

Let's say you're looking at a cheap claiming race for older horses and there is a 7 year old gelding that is getting blinkers in today's race after racing without them in recent races. It is true that the blinkers could make a difference in the horse's performance, but what are the chances that it will make a profound difference and turn a horse that looks lousy on paper into a winner?

In its long career a 7 year old has worn blinkers before and it didn't turn the horse into a champion so it probably won't make a big difference today. Now let's look at a different scenario. Let's say that you're handicapping a maiden race and there is a 3 year old horse that is starting for the second or third time in his career and the trainer is adding blinkers today.

This young horse has never raced with blinkers and the racing game is new to him. Any change, though it may seem slight, may make a big difference. The trainer's stats show that he has added blinkers 25 times in his life and has a 10% win average with a negative ROI (return on investment) when making that move. At first that seems pretty low, but ask yourself this, "How many times did he add the blinkers to a horse like the maiden and how many times did he add them to an older horse?

Don't be misled by that statistic. The most important statistic is that he has won at times when adding blinkers. Don't get excited about equipment changes for older horses but do consider them as a very important factor when handicapping races for younger horses. They lead to some very nice winning tickets.

14.
Horse Racing Handicapping Angles and the Double Class Drop

If you're trying to figure out how to handicap claiming races and what to do about class drops, you're not alone. Horses that are moving down in class are one of those horse racing mysteries that handicappers have struggled with since claiming races were invented. There are no easy answers and nothing is cast in stone, but here are some thoughts.

First of all, how far down the claiming ladder a horse is dropping does make a difference. Years ago when a horse dropped two levels at once, it was considered a very bad sign. Nowadays, since the purses at many tracks have increased a lot, horses drop in class much more often in order to snag a winning purse.

Claiming and training horses is a business. The decisions that are made are almost always financially motivated. Keep that in mind when you're handicapping a claiming race and you'll be able to understand a lot of the moves that the trainers make with their runners. You may see a horse claimed for $10,000 and then start in an $8,000 claimer in its first race for the new trainer.

At first, this doesn't seem to make sense. The owner just bought the horse for $10,000 and is now offering it to the public for $8,000? The first thought is that there is something wrong with the horse and the owner is trying to unload it. It is better to take a $2,000 loss and get rid of a lame or sick horse than to keep paying trainer fees for a horse that won't return any purse money. However, that may not be the case at all.

It may be that the trainer is sharp enough to realize the horse can win at the $8,000 level and the purse will be high enough to get a very quick profit even if the horse is claimed out of the race. The winner's share of the purse may be a lot more than $2,000 and don't forget that since the new owner knows the horse is good enough to win the race, he may also make a nice haul betting on his own horse.

Particularly perplexing is the double drop in class, when a horse goes down two levels in one move. Once again, however, this may be one of the trainer's moves that he has made money on in the past. Look at the statistics for the trainer to see if he has pulled that move before. You'll often find that it's a standard move and he often wins.

15.
The Best Way to Win at the Horse Races When Just Starting Out

If you've ever been to the horse races or an OTB parlor you've probably tried a little flutter on the races. You may have had some beginner's luck and won, but if you kept betting it's almost certain the luck ran out. It always does. While it takes a little luck at anything you do in life in order to be successful, it takes more than luck to win when you bet on horse races.

No matter what you do or how hard you work at being a handicapper, there are no guarantees that you'll win at the races, but there are a few steps you can take to have a better chance. Gambling is fun, but winning is much better, so here are a few tips for your next trip to the race track.

First of all, the fact that you're reading this shows that you're willing to put some effort into making a profit on your wagers. That's a good start. Let's start with money management and this begins before you ever head for the track or betting parlor. Never gamble with money you can't afford to lose. If you make a bet and worry that you might lose because you need that money to pay a bill, then you're sabotaging yourself. Scared money never wins.

So take only what you can comfortably afford to risk and leave the rest at home. Look over a racing form or program before you leave and start planning your betting campaign. How many races are there and how many will you play? It's a good idea to sit out a few because that will force you to choose only the best bets. There is very rarely a good bet in every race.

Let's say you're taking $100 to the races. $20 of that will be spent on admission and other things like a drink and a hot dog. That leaves $80. If there are ten races and you plan on betting on 8 of them, then that means a bet of $10 per race. On the other hand, if you can eliminate four of them it means you can bet $20 per race.

Your best bet if you really are interested in making a profit is the win bet. The reason is that it is usually the pool with the least amount taken out to satisfy the track and also has the least amount of breakage. Don't worry about breakage for now, just know that it is a hidden cost of playing the races and the less you pay, the better.

Which horse should you bet on? This is the big question that millions of people try to solve every day all over the world. The best advice I can give in a limited space is to stick with the horses that are at the lowest odds in the morning line, but you should usually avoid betting on the favorite, the horse with the lowest odds on the tote board. If you can read the form and handicap, that's good, but if not, find a horse that is in the low end of the odds range, say about 3-1.

While handicapping and picking winners consistently takes a lot of work, just sticking with low odds horses and not betting on favorites will often result in a win or two during the day. On a good day you'll come out ahead and on a bad day, you'll know why they call it gambling.

16.
The Double Down or Parlay Bet for Horse Racing

Trying to come out ahead at the races is very difficult, but many people the world over give it a shot every day. If you're one of those prospectors looking for gold at the finish line here are a few thoughts about betting angles that may help. Just remember that betting on horses is a risky business so keep your bets under control and keep it fun.

The straight win bet usually is the best bet because of the high cost of betting. Wagers all come with a price tag known as the takeout and breakage. Breakage is the rounding off of the payout amount to the nearest dime or nickel. It's almost always a dime nowadays which means the bettor pays more in the end. I know it isn't fun or exciting to think about the cost of betting, but if you're practical and give it a little thought, you'll see why it matters if you are serious about coming out ahead.

Sticking with the win bet will help a little, but how can you maximize that even more to have a better chance to have a winning day? There are gadget bets like the pick three that seem like the same kind of deal, pick a winner in a few races and collect. But one of the problems with that is that you may not particularly like any horse in three consecutive races whereas you may like three horses on the card.

There is nothing to stop you from winning the first bet and then putting all your winnings on the next horse that you like, regardless of which race it may be in. It's called a parlay bet and can amount to some very big paydays, providing you can pick two or more winners in a row. That's the rub. You may win a sizable amount on your first bet and lose it all on the next wager. Ouch! On the other hand, hit two good paying win bets in a row and parlay that amount to boot and you've made a nice packet of money.

The big question then becomes whether or not to bet it all or part of it on your third horse? On the other hand, if you're that far ahead, why bet at all? Maybe it's time to quit and head for the barn, as they say. If you can consistently pick winners then the parlay bet makes sense. On the other hand, if you're good at picking long shots, but your strike rate is low, you will have a lot of losing days if you try the parlay.

For maximum profits I think it's best to stick with mid priced horses when parlay betting.

17.
Horse Racing Speed, Pace, Class, and Distance Adjustments for Handicapping Angles

Handicapping angles are situations that produce winners and profits. Similar to spot plays, they can be found now and then, but the horse player has to be patient and wait for the right circumstances to arise. You don't find them on every program or even every day, but when you do spot one, it can be very profitable.

Speed is a useful factor for handicapping, but is often misused. It's tough to make money betting on the horse that appears to be the fastest horse in the race because that is something that's pretty easy to figure and therefore, the crowd is onto it and will bet the speed horse down, especially if that horse has a big edge.

Pace must also be taken into consideration and that has a big impact on speed. One situation that often arises is a horse that scored a big speed figure at a shorter distance and that is now stretching out, as they say, to a longer distance. It may have raced at the popular 6 furlong distance in a sprint and now it is going a mile and a sixteenth. The big question is whether that runner will also score a big figure at the longer distance.

The first place to look for the answer to that question is the class of the race. If the horse in question is moving up in class and fighting tougher foes, it may not be able to have the race its own way and therefore may not be able to settle down and run its own race. That, of course, brings up the matter of pace. What was the pace scenario in the last race?

If the speed horse had an easy race, perhaps setting easy fractions on the front end, or sitting back and benefiting from two other horses that knocked themselves out in a speed duel, then that may have contributed to an artificially high speed figure that may not repeat itself. On the other hand, if it set honest fractions and is bred to handle the mile and a sixteenth, then it may repeat that effort at a longer distance.

The wise handicapper will look at the class of the race, the pace scenario and running style of the speed horse, and the weight that the runner carries. If all those factors point to another big effort and win from the runner, assuming it won't bounce off the big effort, then it will probably be bet down to a ridiculous figure on the odds board so it is no longer an attractive wager. However, and this is how you can benefit from this angle, if that horse was the beneficiary of an artificially high speed figure and today will not be so lucky, you may find a very good bet in another horse that has the qualifications to win, but will be under bet by the crowd who have the stars and that high rating in their eyes.

You'll rarely get a good bet on one of these big speed horses, but will sometimes find one of your best bets wagering against it.

18.
What Are The Best Odds For Horse Racing Bets That Make a Profit

Betting on horse races is a risky busy, but keeping within a certain odds range with your wagers may help you to keep enough of your money long enough to show a profit. Here's a look at a few possible winning strategies. Just remember that you should never bet more than you can "comfortably" afford to lose.

Let's start by talking about losing, since that's what most people do at the races. How do they lose? They usually are a victim of churn and don't even know it. Churn is a term used in the gambling business that means the slow and relentless loss of money by the player and acquisition of money by the gambling venue due to the take out. In other words, if you pay 18% of your bet every time you make a win bet at the races, you are automatically down 18% each time. If you pay 18% win or lose every time you wager, it eventually eats your bankroll unless you can average more than 18% profit. Think about that.

That's one very good reason to limit your wagers and to try to get big enough payoffs, high enough odds, so that you don't have to play too often or win too often. The odds range that seems to fit that criteria is between 3-1 and 8-1. The reasons are that most of the winners at the track, other than the favorites who win about 30% of the time, are in that odds range.

Also, the horses that are second, third, and fourth in the morning line are usually within that range and so are the bettor's choices when the real gambling begins. You'll find most of your winners in that group and confining your efforts to horses in that range will help you to cash often enough to stay in the game, as long as you can also do a bit of handicapping.

It may be nice to bet on long shots and to cash big winning tickets, but it seldom happens unless you have a good method for picking live horses at long odds. It is a common mistake to think that the best overlays, horses that are a good bet because the crowd has underestimated them, are long shots. A horse that will win a third of the time that's going to post at 5-1 is a fantastic bet because you will double your money if you stick to that kind of bet when the horse is that good.

It does happen, but rarely. Seasoned handicappers won't let a good horse with a realistic chance of winning go to post at very long odds, but sometimes you can make a profit on the mid range odds horses because the casual bettors at the race track will load up on a favorite that isn't as good as they think it is.

I hope you enjoyed these simple horse racing articles and thoughts. You'll find some of my books in the Kindle Owners Lending Library where you may borrow them for free. The Kindle Unlimited program also features some of these books. Please remember, for more in-depth handicapping lessons and ideas you can read my full length handicapping books in the *Horseplayer Series,* available at Amazon. My books not only teach valuable handicapping lessons, but also share advice about being a horseplayer…

You'll find a complete list of my books at my Amazon Authors page at…
http://www.amazon.com/Bill-Peterson/e/B0044XE19A/

You'll find interesting horse racing handicapping systems at
http://williewins.homestead.com/handicappingstore.html

Enjoy your days at the races,

Bill Peterson

Printed in Poland
by Amazon Fulfillment
Poland Sp. z o.o., Wrocław